W9-BXY-623

History
with a Twist

History with a Twist

Unusual Stories from
Mr. Nova Scotia Know-It-All
Bruce Nunn

NIMBUS
PUBLISHING

Nimbus Publishing Limited
PO Box 9301, Station A
Halifax, NS   B3K 5N5
(902)455-4286

Design: Margaret Issenman

Printed and bound by Printcrafters Inc.

CANADIAN CATALOGUING IN PUBLICATION DATA
Nunn, Bruce, 1962 -
History with a Twist
Includes bibliographical references.
ISBN 1-55109-255-7
1. Nova Scotia — History. 2. Tales — Nova Scotia.   I. Title.
GR113.5.N69N85 1998   971.6   C98-950158-2

Nimbus Publishing acknowledges the financial support of the Canada Council and the Department of Canadian Heritage.

Contents

Foreword

To twist, just a tad, the content and the intent of the wondrous William Butler Yeats:

All the words that we utter,
Must spread out their wings untiring,
And never rest in their flight,
Til they come where your glad, glad heart is,
And sing to you in the night (or morning)
Beyond where the traffic is moving,
Storm-darken'd or starry bright.

Problem is… with radio, in nanoseconds, wonderful stories are released into the ether and dispersed throughout the cosmos never to be relished again; never to be heard again in a way that a favourite print story might continue to delight for a lifetime.

In a longish period of working in radio—longer than I'm prepared to admit—I have been struck hundreds of times by the sad thought that moments of great import as well as moments of great fun have disappeared beyond Uranus. For some time I have been encouraging Bruce to take the time to prevent his stories from suffering the same fate. He resisted, then he relented, and we are delighted. Mr. Nova Scotia Know-It-All stories have been a welcome addition to *Information Morning*, not only because they have resurrected important elements of our history but also because they have been graced with Bruce's unique (peculiar?) sensibility.

After you've read this book, lend it to a friend. Send it to a child. These are some stories from our heartland told with art and affection. And most of them are primarily true!

Don Connolly
Information Morning
CBC Radio One, Mainland, Nova Scotia

Preface

Or, "I'd like to thank everyone I've ever met."

"Oh, you're that Know-It-All guy on the radio!" If only I had a *Bluenose* dime for each time I've heard that statement in the last three years. I am repeatedly amazed at the number of Nova Scotians who listen intently, enthusiastically and daily to CBC Radio's *Information Morning*, weekdays, between 6:00 and 9:00 AM. Loyal listeners all. I sometimes wonder how a morning show host copes with such scrutiny, even as friendly as it is. Personally, I don't know how to respond to it. I'm really not a Know-It-All at all, I just play one on the radio. But let me say I am honoured, flattered and more than a little surprised by the keen interest that Nova Scotians have shown in this little storytelling gig we've created on the airwaves. I say "we" because the birth of this phenomenon of Know-It-All-ism was attended by many midwives. It was a very short labour. I was minding my own business one day at CBC Radio, working that summer as the field reporter for *Information Morning*. Hard news. Current affairs. Serious stuff. *Real* journalism. But the program's producer that summer, my friend Ron Sherrard, decided we needed something more. In his practical, creative way, he came up with the idea of a weekly feature. Something regular to inform, entertain— and fill a time slot. Solid summer programming. Know-It-Alling was Ron's idea. Now you have someone to blame. But as often happens around that magical radio shop, the idea spread, with others fanning the flames. Ron said, "Answer listeners' questions." Stewart Young said, "Yeah, but just Nova Scotia questions." Kelly Ryan said, "We could call you 'The Nova Scotia Know-It-All!' " She liked the alliteration of "Nova" and "Know it." "I've got the perfect, cheesy theme music for the item," Ron exclaimed. I didn't get a vote. Later, it was dear Don Connolly who tagged my already absurd title with the saucy "Mr." Hence, Know-It-All-ism was personified!

A game show treatment was created to enliven what could have otherwise been a boring history segment. I guess I took the mandate at face value and fell into a natural habit of injecting humour and odd approaches to the storytelling. Don helped craft the character. All that aside, none of us knew what we were tapping into. I discovered a goldmine of amazing, poignant, dramatic, funny, and fascinating stories. In Nova Scotia, the truth is better than fiction. The culture of this place is like wonderful wooden folk art—warm, witty, colourful and solid—carved with character and history in every line.

I also tapped into an inner love of "story." Everyone who works in or listens to radio loves a good story. Nova Scotia has them, and I like to tell them. Call it historical journalism. I'm glad to play a part in reflecting people's culture back to them, to spread their tales to fellow Nova Scotians. I learned how to tell stories from two young but powerful influences in my life, my sons. Their nightly demand, "tell us a story from your mouth," rather than from a book, helped me hone a skill I never knew I had. Thomas Nathaniel and Adam Joseph deserve a lot of thanks. Thanks guys. Here's the book we always talked about making one day, and you helped!

This book is a collection of stories unique to Nova Scotia. They were all previously told on and adapted from CBC Radio One's *Information Morning* program. Some are longer. Some are shorter. Most of them are fleshed out with added detail and personal reflection not permitted by radio's time limits. The shorter radio tales contained here have appeared in an edited form in my biweekly newspaper column in the *Chronicle Herald* and *Mail Star* newspapers. The column is currently in the *Sunday Herald*.

My writing style here is consistent, I hope, with the tone of the Know-It-All radio versions (read: slightly twisted.) All of these are true stories, researched in as much detail as possible within the scope of media deadlines. These tales originated from suggestions by faithful CBC radio listeners around the province. Folks write, e-mail, phone, and fax the CBC questions about things Nova Scotian in nature. One gentleman even dropped by with a yellowed wartime newspaper he thought I could cull for interesting stories!

I owe a big thank you to the following folks who have helped me sound like I really do know it all: the helpful reference staff at the Halifax

Regional Library; Garry Shutlak at Nova Scotia Archives and Records Management; Dan Conlin and his mates at the Maritime Museum of the Atlantic; Terry Punch, expert genealogist; and Allan Doyle at the Nova Scotia Department of Tourism. Many thanks to provincial trivia king, Dave Harley; film expert, Ron Foley MacDonald; Gaelic coach, Lewis MacKinnon; dramatic reader, George Jordan; computer contributor and Internet consultant, Costas Halavrezos. Also, I am grateful to all the museum workers around the province who respond to my information requests. I give a special nod to all of the helpful contacts I have made around the province—the folks I have met over the phone, and the others I hope to meet soon. They are the numerous amateur historians, family history buffs, curious newspaper clippers and the good old-fashioned community elders who keep memories alive and preserve the stories of our past.

In writing this book I am deeply indebted to two talented friends who were my editors: Nancy O'Donnell and Ron Sherrard. Without their help, this book would be riddelled with a merriad of atroshus spellin erors. Without their skilled guidance, my writing would have suffered from awkwardly contorted and, I guess, some might say awry, or perhaps weakly-structured sentences that just plain didn't work good; like a round tire that doesn't roll because it's not really very round. Thanks to you both for your superior editing efforts during a very busy winter. By the way, if the reader should happen to spot a rare spelling error any-where in this book, congratulations! We left a few there on purpose. To test you. Yeah, that's it, it's a test... though there's really no need to call and report them! I also reserve a special place of profound gratitude in my heart for my translator, John O'Donnell, who patiently explained to me what the heck it was that my computer was trying to say to me. Many late nights I struggled to understand its hidden logic. I could sense an intelligence deep inside there somewhere, but I lacked the technical strength to reach it. John helped, God bless him. My thanks also to the good folks at Nimbus Publishing who approached me about producing a story collection adapted from CBC Radio.

A tip of the sou'wester to Stewart, Don and crew at the good ship *Information Morning.* To my fellow CBC shipmates who ply the same (air)waves, thanks for your interest in these stories. A special salute to Jane Merchant at CBC Halifax. A final word of gratitude to my mother, Nora (McKenna) Nunn who helped give me an appreciation of the ties that bind our people in this maritime culture. I believe that her gift combined with the radio heritage inherited from my father helped me craft my peculiar brand of on-air storytelling.

I hope you enjoy reading this collection of Mr. Nova Scotia Know-It-All stories as much as I've enjoyed meeting the publishing deadline!

N. Bruce Nunn
(Mr. N.S.K.I.A.)

Just Plaid to Be Here!

Investigating illegal Nova Scotia tartan.

O ut of the blue I had a call from a lawyer. A call from a lawyer is like seeing flashing police lights in your rearview mirror. You know you've done nothing wrong, but you feel instantly guilty anyway. What could she want? Why me? Not to worry. This time, it was about what *I* could do for *her*. The lawyer, that is. You see, this lawyer represented a whole bunch of other lawyers. (What is the proper word, a "brief" of lawyers? Perhaps an "objection" of lawyers?) The Canadian Bar Association had designated a certain day as "Law Day" across the country. I guess they have the power to do that. This local legal eagle wanted me to research an interesting angle to one of Nova Scotia's laws, to promote "Law Day." "Sure," I said, "for $165 an hour." She didn't laugh. (I guess that rules out a "giggle" of lawyers.) Anyway, she suggested I investigate the law concerning the Nova Scotia tartan. I said I'd be "plaid" to.

I didn't even question that there was a law, enacted by our legislature, governing something as natural and ubiquitous as our beautiful blue Nova Scotia tartan. What a grand province we live in! Something as harmless as tartan would, of course, require strict legal controls. Makes perfect sense. Lock it down tightly! God knows what kind of tartan trouble we'd have on our hands without rigid restrictions! Actually, God might know, but frankly I didn't. "Why," I asked the good lawyer, "do we have a Nova Scotia tartan law?" Apparently that was for her to know and me to find out. I was on the case.

First I investigated the background of our provincial tartan. It just wouldn't do if our official plaid had a checkered past. The Nova Scotia tartan, I learned, is made from carefully chosen symbolic colours: the blue of the sea; a light and a dark green for our trees, evergreen and deciduous; the white stripe, for the ocean surf; yellow-gold representing the province's Royal Charter; and the red line representing a… red lion.

How punfully appropriate. The red stripe stands for the Heraldic red "lion rampant" gracing the centre of the Nova Scotia flag. All this quaint symbolism makes for a beautiful tartan. But this tartan is a legally controlled substance, like alcohol, subject to a statute of the Nova Scotia provincial legislature. It's called *An Act Respecting the Nova Scotia Tartan*—and it's still on the books.

The Act was passed in 1963 and updated in 1990, so someone still cares. It controls the making and distribution of our pretty blue Nova Scotia tartan as though it were a mind-altering drug or counterfeit money. Luckily, I found a lawyer who would tell me about this law, free of charge. David Coles pulled a thick book of statutes from a long aisle of floor-to-ceiling law books at his Dartmouth office.

"It's an offense in Nova Scotia," he explained, "to sell tartan that hasn't been licensed by the government, either for its manufacture or sale."

Section six, subsection two of the *Nova Scotia Tartan Act* reads as follows: "No person shall sell or offer for sale the Tartan or any article to which the design of the Tartan has been applied unless the Tartan or the article to which the design of the Tartan has been applied was manufactured by a person granted a licence pursuant to Section 5 and which has marked upon or attached thereto the name 'Nova Scotia Tartan' or such other identifying mark as has been approved by the Minister of Tourism and Culture."

A sample of illegal Nova Scotia tartan. Can you tell the difference?

"It's also an offense to pass off other material that looks like our tartan," Coles declared. "Even mock tartan is illegal?" I gasped. Yup! Section six, subsection four: "No person shall sell or offer for sale any woven material so closely resembling the Tartan as to be mistaken for the Tartan."

Well, I guess you wouldn't want to get a bad batch. So, anyone who makes or sells Nova Scotia tartan ties, boxer shorts, vests, ribbons, or jammies needs a licence. If you are an illegal tartan trafficker—a plaid pusher—you face a $500 fine. However, there are plenty of plaid pedlars in the province, but only one officially sanctioned Nova Scotia tartan dealer. All the rest are illegally tartanizing!

Before I name names, a word about how our provincial tartan came about. It was born of a mix of handicraft, political craft, and corporate capitalism. Surprisingly, perhaps, it began not with a Scot, but a Nova Scotian Englishwoman. In 1953, a weaver named Bessie Baily Murray was asked to create a fabric display for the Nova Scotia Sheep Breeders Association's booth at a Farm and Fisheries Exhibition in Truro. These rural provincial exhibitions are an annual tradition. They usually feature demonstrations of different developments in our primary industries: fishing, farming, and forestry. They're also a good place to step in cow manure, a memorable part of the fair experience.

Mrs. Murray and her team of handy crafters created a fourteen-foot fabric mural for the Sheep Breeder's exhibition display. It depicted a pastoral scene of a Nova Scotian Highlander on a hill, tending his sheep with a glimpse of shoreline in the distance. The fabric creation was meant to represent the Highland culture which cherishes the symbols and ways of their homeland: bagpipes, the kilt, and

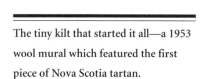

The tiny kilt that started it all—a 1953 wool mural which featured the first piece of Nova Scotia tartan.

living off the land. But Bessie Murray didn't want to start a clan war by her choice of tartan for the wee shepherd's kilt. Different Highland clans are represented by different colours and very specific plaid designs. How could she choose Chisholm over MacDonald, or MacKay over MacKenzie? Instead, she created a tiny kilt reflecting the new homeland of these Highland Scots. The fabulous fabric panel she crafted now hangs in the Barrington Woollen Mill Museum in Shelburne County.

Bessie's tartan design was just a couple of inches wide on that wee shepherd's kilt. However, it stood out, because of what it stood for. Folks began to ask about it, and for it. A few hand-crafted items were made from the new tartan. The plaid's popularity progressed. All it needed was the official seal of approval. The design had to be registered according to Scottish rules.

The Highland heritage of Premier Angus L. Macdonald was exploited. The province's Director of Handcrafts, Mary Black, brought Bessie Murray's plaid to Angus L., as he was casually known. He was smitten and suggested that Bessie weave several designs for his scrutiny. She did. Macdonald chose the one he liked and presented it to Cabinet. The plaid was also presented to Angus L.'s friend, the Lord Lyon, King of Arms in Scotland—the man with the power to grant official tartan status to a plaid. The politics of plaidness! Meanwhile here at home, the Attorney General's Department personally handled Bessie's application for Canadian copyright of her design, under her name. Officialdom satisfied, Bessie's new company, Nova Scotia Tartan Ltd., began hand-weaving Nova Scotia tartan. Premier Angus L. got a new scarf out of the deal. Years later, just before the copyright ran out, the province made the blue tartan an official part of the Heraldic Armorial Bearings of Nova Scotia in the *Nova Scotia Tartan Act*. So it was right up there with the flag and the crest—out of the public domain for good.

Entrepreneurs hoping to sell the newly protected tartan to bagpipers or Scottish dancers were required to pay the government an annual fee. He who kilted the piper paid the province.

Eventually, a Dutch industrialist in Yarmouth took over the Nova Scotia tartan business and purchased the first and only official tartan licence from the Crown. I discovered an odd parallel between the licence and British spy movies. The licence number was NS1- double-'O'-1 (a "license to kilt"?) The company's name, believe it or not, is Bonda. The Bonda business was sold in the fall of 1996. I happened to call the new owner, John Cluley, on the day he was designing aggressive new labels for his tartan products.

"In changing the labels," he told me, "I was thinking that we should be saying '*licensed* Nova Scotia tartan,' since we were the original licensee of the product."

The official tartan of the Highland Games? Well, not exactly. But the Bonda plant remains the only licensed and legal Nova Scotia tartan distributor. Surprisingly, Bonda doesn't weave its own supply of our lovely blue tartan. In fact, hardly any of the ubiquitous blue is woven here in the province. Bonda imports its big blue bolts from West Coast Woollen Mills in Vancouver, British Columbia. Farewell to Nova Scotia! Our tartan comes from that *other* seabound coast!

I was so amazed I couldn't even heave a sigh or a wish. What's worse, I checked into the BC mill's legal status and discovered that they actually don't have a licence to kilt! They are bad plaiders. They are illegal tartan traffickers, dealing in Celtic contraband and operating from the west coast. But we have no tartan police to enforce the law, so these west coast weavers are getting off… Scot free.

This kind of criminal activity is apparently widespread. I talked with a tartanizer who has been in the biz for a long time. Charles Clerk of Island Beach Ltd. operates a local chain of clothing stores. He openly admits he has no licence for his Nova Scotia tartan T-shirts, underwear, caps, keytags, and stuffed lobsters. According to Clerk, illegal tartanizers circle the globe.

"[The Nova Scotia tartan] is probably made by every Asian country, the United States, Mexico.… I know it's produced in Scotland, England, Germany, and Ireland. You'll even see it on the fashion runways in New York." And none of them have a Nova Scotia tartan licence. Shame, shame. Mr. Clerk didn't seem remorseful either.

When I called West Coast Woollen Mills to find out who else they were supplying, their spokesperson didn't even know that our tartan is a legally controlled substance. She offered to send me a free, illegal tartan sample if I faxed her a copy of our tartan law. So we swapped, one for the other. My swatch of illegal Nova Scotia tartan now adorns my coffee table. I hope I don't get busted for possession.

Of Wooden Ships and Irony, Men

A century-old, Nova Scotian wreck-and-rescue story.

It was the best of times. It was the worst of times.

During the post-Dickensian days of the 1880s, a seaman's life was rugged, ragged, and adventurous. Nova Scotians, born and raised with their salty sea heritage, knew the dangers and dramas of distant waters. Small crews of flesh-and-bone men set out on bobbing vessels of wood; insignificant specs on the planet's vast, churning oceans. Risk was a way of life. Survival often hung on luck and prayer. Have you ever watched a tiny bug riding a splinter of wood down a swirling gutter drain? It seems so ridiculously minuscule compared to our complex human lives. But imagine a mariner's life a hundred years ago. Sailors clinging to bundles of wood and canvas lashed together by ropes. Men who braved the unforgiving depths of the sea, fighting the unpredictable power of nature. And when brutal storms struck hard, sailors had no choice but to hold on and pray. No control. No turning back. At the mercy of uncaring seas. Year after year, Nova Scotian sailors gambled for their lives and for their livelihood. It was what they knew. It was a way of life—and sometimes a way of death. This story is about one of those dramas. It began with a phone call.

On a crisp winter morning, CBC Radio program host Don Connolly, and I had finished our usual jousting of on-air wit; something he and I do weekly (or should I say "weakly"?). The latest "Know-It-All" story had gone out on the air waves to the minds and memories of Nova Scotian listeners. A mere saunter from the studio, down the hall, the phone in the newsroom was already ringing. Only a minute earlier, we had announced the phone numbers for the "Know-It-All Hotline." Ahh, the magic of radio! Jane Fraser-Deveau was phoning from her Halifax home before leaving for work. She wanted me to look into the life of her great-grandfather, the rugged but unlucky Captain Marmaduke Fraser. What a name! That's usually a good clue to a great story; a name that sounds like a Hollywood invention. Jane said that Marmaduke was a sea captain from Tatamagouche. He sailed the *Indian Chief*, an ill-fated vessel embroiled in an unforgettable and deadly ordeal in wild English Channel waters in 1881. His ship floundered, with horrible consequences, in a fierce gale at the infamous Goodwin Sands. Captain Marmaduke Fraser's great-granddaughter wanted to share this unbelievable shipwreck story with me. But she also wanted to enlist my help. She hoped I might confirm her own research and perhaps uncover more about her relative.

I arranged to meet with Jane Fraser-Deveau at her Halifax house. Spry, smiling and curious, she was a grown-up version of that other Jane, from 1950s and 60s elementary school readers. Remember Dick and Jane? Both Janes, I think, shared an enthusiasm for learning new things. In fact, Jane Fraser-Deveau had learned, quite by accident, that her great-grandfather's shipwreck story was still recounted by some fine folk in Britain. She made that discovery in 1978. Here's how in the Dick and Jane style:

Jane journeyed to England. See Jane journey. Journey Jane, journey! Jane was in London. See the big clock! She was tired. She spotted a pub. See Jane spot! Jane went in the pub. She saw a stranger. The stranger said, "Why are you in England, Jane?" Jane told him her story. The stranger was a fireman. He knew Jane's story! Jane was lucky. Lucky Jane. It was exciting.

Here's the grown-up version. Jane began by telling me what she told the stranger in the pub:

"We're here because of my great-grandfather, Marmaduke Fraser, who went down with his ship *Indian Chief* on the Goodwin Sands."

"Oh, know it well! Know the story well!" Jane mimicked the fireman's surprising reply, complete with accent.

Jane was skeptical, but the stranger's reply wasn't just a beer-hall boast.

"I came to find out this man was a fireman," said Jane, "and he knew a great deal about rescues, and it just so happened that this was one of

A rescue boat tries to reach the *Indian Chief* going down in the English Channel.

the rescues that he'd studied. It is one of the best known stories of lifeboat rescues."

Of all the gin joints in all the world, Jane had to walk into *this* one. What a confluence of coincidence! Jane learned that her great-grandfather's name is well known in England's nautical safety circles. And so is his brother's name, Primrose Fraser. Another great name. More evidence of a dramatic story ahead—Primrose happened to be on the same doomed vessel.

The *Indian Chief*, two hundred feet long, and 1,238 tonnes, was built in 1877 in Quebec. Her stern ornament was a silhouetted head of a North American indian chief, finished in gold on black. Laden with general cargo, *Indian Chief*, with her Nova Scotian captain and his brother as second mate, had twenty-nine souls on board when she sailed out of Middlesborough, England headed for Yokohama, Japan. But she never made it out of the English Channel.

The rest of this story is the kind of drama that makes a spellbinding historical novel: tragedy, danger, and heroism, all rolled into one.

Three days into their voyage, Captain Marmaduke Fraser and his crew ran into trouble. The weather had been thick and threatening since the Sunday afternoon they left port. By Wednesday morning at 2:30 AM, they had entered the maze of hidden shoals and sunken sandbars that are infamous to Channel sailors. The wind shifted. A sudden squall of rain blew up. It was very dark. The wind increased to gale force. The ship drifted towards the Long Sand at Kentish Knock. Captain Marmaduke ordered her about. But the main braces tangled. The spanker boom sheet fouled the wheel at a critical moment. Confusion reigned. The vessel heeled sharply. She struck the ground broadside

Rowing rescuers fought stormy swells to reach the wreck of the *Indian Chief*.

with a terrible shudder. The vessel was stuck, upright, grounded on the sand with wild, howling winds whipping through the rigging. Waves rolled higher and higher against the hull.

The men prepared a flare and sent up rockets. Their signals were answered by responding flares from a distant light-ship. Their position was known! The men knew that their vessel, stuck hard and fast, would likely leave its wooden bones on that sand, but they didn't plan to die. In the light of the flares, the crew could see one another's determined faces. They sang cheerily, to keep their spirits up while they waited for help to come. Later, the first mate of the *Indian Chief*, William Lloyd, gave graphic descriptions of the crew's ordeal to *The Daily Telegraph* newspaper, in London:

"All this while, the wind was gradually sweeping up into a gale—and oh, the cold, good Lord! The bitter cold of that wind!"

The men's hearts leapt when they caught sight of a sail. They rushed to the side and stared, the salt spray whitening their faces like a layer of flour as they watched, unblinking, so as not to lose sight for an instant. But the distant boat couldn't fight the huge seas. She turned and went away. The gale grew more fierce.

"As we lay broadside, on to the waves, the sheets of flying water soon made the sloping decks a dangerous place for a man to stand on and the crew and officers kept the shelter of the deck-cabins."

Marmaduke, his brother, Primrose, and William Lloyd, constantly ventured from their cabins on to the flooded deck to check for rescue boats. None could be seen. Nothing was visible in the rainy maelstrom that night. Morning broke but the storm blew as strongly as ever. The ship strained with the force of the waves.

"Every moment threatened to bring the spars crashing down about us, and the thundering and beating of the canvas made the masts buckle and jump like fishing rods."

Marmaduke ordered three boats launched. One boat was instantly engulfed by waves and sank with two men in her. "The poor fellows in her vanished just as you might blow out a light." The two other boats filled and sank as soon as they touched the water. The crew was trapped on board the *Indian Chief*, with no help in sight. The dreadful ordeal continued throughout the long, dark day. Near five o'clock, a huge sea swept over, taking the deck houses. The ship broke her back. The hull filled. The wooden boards of the deck were blown through and great yawning openings showed the dark water rising. Marmaduke ordered the men to take to the mizen-mast thinking it was the safest place to be. Unfortunately, he was wrong.

᷈

The miserable sailors, soaked and cold, climbed up into the rigging and the wooden crosstrees of the vessel. They cut pieces of line to lash themselves to the thick mast. The wind tried to weaken their hold. Others scaled the foremast. They too lashed themselves in tightly.

Primrose Fraser showed great courage. A stout twenty-two-year-old, he was strapped in next to his brother. William Lloyd was near too, at the top of the mizen-mast. Lloyd had high regard for the second mate. "As fine a specimen of the 'English' sailor as ever I was shipmate with. He was calling about him cheerfully, bidding us not be downhearted, and telling us to look sharply around for the lifeboats. He helped some of the benumbed men lash themselves, saying encouraging things to them as he made them fast."

Marmaduke equalled his brother's calm and courage in the face of death. The captain, knowing he might go down with his ship, was thinking of his family back in Tatamagouche.

"The Captain shook hands with me," said Lloyd to *The Telegraph*, "and on the chance of my being saved, gave me some messages to take home, too sacred to be written down. He handed me his watch and chain and I put them in my pocket."

The scene had shades of the crucifixion. High up, on the cross-piece of a wooden mast, Marmaduke was lashed, forsaken, pierced by spears of driving, freezing rain, knowing he would probably die, speaking final words to his seafaring disciple, to be passed on to loved ones after he was gone.

The men hung on for dear life, though the life within them was dwindling. Night fell. A weak moon barely lit the darkness. The winds were relentless. Streams of torn canvas overhead flapped like a continuous roll of thunder. William Lloyd said that "the men hung in the topmast rigging like corpses. The wind went through our skins like showers of arrows." Young Primrose Fraser tried to shelter his brother, Marmaduke, by curving his own body against the winds.

A sudden fancy entered William Lloyd's head. A "sort of craze" struck him, a sudden fearful eagerness to leave the mizen-mast. He called to the captain but heard no reply. Looking down to the swirling, swamped deck below, he knew going down meant drowning. "Every sea that rolled over the wreck left less of her than it found." The first mate left the captain and his brother and climbed into the cross-trees. He inched hand-over-hand down one of the topmast stays and found a secured rope. He reached the foremast and lashed himself in with the nine or ten other men who were there. William's fingers were skinned and numb. The light-ship sent up signal rockets every hour, but there was still no sign of rescue. Not in that torrent.

William clung to the foremast; Marmaduke and his brother clung to the mizen-mast. Time crawled by. The storm continued unabated into the night. Then William saw tragedy follow disaster.

"It was now about three o'clock on Thursday morning; the air was full of the strange dim light of the foam and the stars and I could very plainly see the black swarm of men in the top and rigging of the mizen-mast. I was looking that way when a great sea fell upon the hull of the ship with a fearful crash; a moment after, the mainmast went. It fell quickly and, as it fell, it bore down the mizen-mast. There was a horrible noise of splintering wood and some piercing cries and then another great sea swept over the afterdeck and we who were in the foretop looked and saw the stumps of the two masts sticking up from the bottom of the hold, the mizen-mast slanting over the bulwarks into the water and the men lashed to it, drowning."

They were tied and underwater. The first mate watched his ship-mates drowning from his perch on the foremast, a perch he had chosen as an afterthought. It had been a gamble. As sailors they all knew that the mainmast, in the centre of the three, would give way first once the ship's hull broke her back. It was a guessing game which way it would fall—whether it would take out the foremast or the mizen-mast. It was a life-and-death gamble with 50-50 odds. William's second-guessing saved his life. His captain and many mates made an unlucky choice. Now they were gone. Only grief and the cold remained. The lone foremast stood erect against the furious force of the gale. But it rocked and shook in a fearful manner. Another dawn broke. Miraculously, the remaining men were still clinging to the foremast—clinging to life—as the seas churned like a boiling cauldron. All hope was drowned, like the swirling mass of bodies tangled in the toppled rigging. Devastation and desperation were all that remained. The first mate gave up hope. He waited his turn to die.

Then a loud cry. William turned his head. A lifeboat! There—then gone. Huge, rising and falling waves. There it was again. My God, a lifeboat!

"It was a sight, sir, to make one crazy with joy and it put the strength of ten men into every one of us."

The lifeboat rose high in the sky, then dropped out of sight, emerging again and again, plodding towards the desperate men. "By this time we knew that this boat was here to save us and that she *would* save us and, with wildly beating hearts, we unlashed ourselves and dropped over the top into the rigging."

As sailors they knew what needed to be done. They lashed together ropes to create a line, tied a piece of wood to one and tossed it into the waves for the lifeboat men. Two shipmates shinnied out on the fallen mizen-mast to recover the body of Primrose Fraser. They pulled him into the lifeboat. The courageous coxswain, commander of the lifeboat, was a man ably fitted for the job, by skill and by name. The first mate recounted the leader's first orders on the scene.

"I heard the coxswain of the boat—Charles Fish by name—cry out, 'Take that poor fellow in there!' and he pointed to the body of the captain, who was lashed in the top with his arms over the mast and his head erect and his eyes wide open. But one of our crew called out, 'He's been dead four hours, sir.' And then the rest of us scrambled into the boat, looking away from the dreadful group of drowned men that lay in a cluster round the prostrate mast. The second mate was still alive, but a maniac; it was heartbreaking to hear his broken, feeble cries for his brother but he lay quiet after a bit and died in half an hour, though we chafed his feet and poured rum in his mouth and did what men in our miserable plight could for a fellow sufferer."

The lucky eleven surviving sailors had escaped their first miserable ordeal. There was yet a second ordeal to survive. A terrorizing trip to shore. "The broken water was enough to turn a man's hair grey to look at it." The surviving men were now riding on the wild surface of the roiling sea that they had been looking down upon from their high perches. William Lloyd remembered thinking he might not make it. "I felt almost as though I should have been safer on the wreck than in that boat." The lifeboat rose as high as a house and fell, climbed another great crest, then disappeared again. Up and down, the open lifeboat rode the gigantic waves. Finally, finally, the safety of shore! It was over. But their minds still reeled with the memories of their shipmates' catastrophic end.

The human tragedy of the *Indian Chief*'s wreck left a legacy of courage. Captain Marmaduke Fraser and his brother Primrose were remembered with respect and awe at their perseverance in the face of nature's onslaught.

～

The terrible drama was well recorded by the press of the day. The *Daily Telegraph* reported the surviving first mate's vivid descriptions in detail. Like reports in Nova Scotia of the infamous Moose River Mine disaster, this nautical tragedy captured the public's imagination and has remained in their memories. As for Coxswain Charles Fish of the rescue boat, his bravery earned him a gold medal, presented by His Royal Highness, the Duke of Edinburgh on behalf of the Royal National Lifeboat Institution—a voluntary marine rescue organization in Britain that has been around since 1824. The RNLI recounted this saga in August 1915, in the Journal of the Royal National Lifeboat Institution, on the occasion of the brave coxswain's death. That's why, when the captain's great-granddaughter, Jane Fraser-Deveau, bumped into that fireman in a London pub, he was already familiar with the story. I called the Royal National Lifeboat Institution in Poole, England. It turned out that the *Indian Chief*'s sea saga is indeed very well known. The ship's wooden stern ornament, the carved head of an Indian Chief, resides in a museum in Ramsgate, England. Those in British rescue circles learn about this classic rescue at their old institution. But the British didn't have the whole story. At least not about Marmaduke's loved ones to whom his last words were addressed.

The great-granddaughter of that iron-blooded sea captain, discovered something that made her wonder exactly what those last words might have been. Jane Fraser-Deveau was amused to learn from an elder relative in Nova Scotia, that the salty sea captain, Marmaduke Fraser, had won her great-grandmother in a poker game. Apparently, on one of Marmaduke's visits to Tokyo he ended up in a heated poker game with the girl's father. Low on coin, the man threw his own daughter into the poker pot.

"He said that Marmaduke could have her if he lost the next hand, and sure enough he did. And so Marmaduke actually won my great-grandmother in a poker game, and immediately took her to sea for almost a year! They went off to India and she absolutely hated him! So, I'm not so sure that she minded him going down with his ship!" Jane chuckled.

What a twist! Marmaduke had won his wife in a poker game but not her heart. In the end, his loss was her gain.

↬

One final twist: Primrose Fraser, Marmaduke's brother, was commemorated in a special way too. The coxswain of that Royal National Lifeboat Institution's rescue boat was so inspired by the spirit of the *Indian Chief*'s brave second mate, that he named his own child after the Nova Scotian sailor. The newborn's name? "Primrose Fish."

The Bigfoot in Nova Scotia's Woods

A woodsman with huge feet and a heart to match.

Some say he towered over seven feet tall. He left giant footprints in the snow. People in the Salmon River area of Digby County called him "*Gros Pieds.*" In English, he was known as "Bigfoot," but he wasn't the legendary beast from the Tibetan mountains. He was a very human Bigfoot. Born January 24, 1908, Joseph Alphée Deveau, a tall and likeable Nova Scotian Acadian woodsman had—well… there's no nice way to say this—he had humongous hoofers! Huge, gigantic feet! Sure, he was a tall man—his actual height was 6 ft. 4 in.—and his long, lean body was perfectly proportioned, except from his ankles down. It was not your ordinary genetic abnormality.

Alphée's appearance was unremarkable until you looked down at his big black leather boots. Let's just say he would have been an outstanding attraction at a podiatrist convention. Relatives told me that Alphée Deveau's feet were sixteen inches long, five inches wide and about six inches thick. That's a lot of inches in a foot. They say he wore a size 24 shoe. You could say he stood on his principles. But, behind those startling foot facts, there lies a touching tale. Because, in addition to his unavoidably noticeable large feet, Alphée Deveau had an even bigger heart.

I first heard about Nova Scotia's Bigfoot from Margaret Veneau in the early days of CBC Radio's Mr. Know-It-All. She phoned to ask me to tell his story. I did some research and discovered that *Gros Pieds* had relatives living in Dartmouth. Henry Deveau was *Gros Pieds*'s cousin, who once lived across the road from him in Salmon River, just north of Yarmouth. Henry's wife Kay remembered Alphée too. They were both glad to talk about him. They liked him and it turns out that everybody who knew *Gros Pieds* liked him too. Henry went straight to the soul of the story—Alphée's soles.

"He had to have his boots specially made at the shoemaker shop at Saulnierville," Henry said. Saulnierville is about fifteen miles from Salmon River. That's the length he had to go to get his feet fitted. "No store sold a boot that size. And if you go to some places in the States, you will still see his boot in the shops of some shoemakers because he had a lot of relations." I suppose any shoemaker asked to fit such a footing would be impressed. Naturally, they'd want to keep a sample shoe to show. Quite a spectacular window display. In Ed Sullivan-speak, you might call it "A rully big shoe!" The thing that sticks out in the mind of Henry Deveau's wife, Kay, was the big toe that stuck out from each of Alphée's enormous feet; a protuberance so prominent that podiatrists panicked.

"His big toe was humongous! He would take his shoe off and show the kids," she said. "One time he was in the woods and he cut his big toe with an axe. The cut was about an inch deep and it still didn't show the bone!" Eewwwww. That's more than I wanted to hear. But, for the sake of the story, I took a giant step. "How *big* was it," I asked, "the size

Nova Scotia's gentle bigfoot, Alphée Deveau.

of a golf ball? The size of an apple?" Kay's answer surprised me. "It was the size of my fist anyway," she said. "It was big! It was huge!"

It occurred to me that his feet must have been a tremendous advantage to him as a woodsman. In a time before steel-toed boots, the natural padding up front must have kept Alphée from doing more damage to his foot than he might have. Axe-idents happen. And tramping through the woods in winter, with feet as long and as wide as snowshoes, must have made a logger's life a little easier. But it was a tough trail through life for this shy man, whose feet stood out although he didn't want to. Alphée lived a quiet and simple life in a small community.

"Strangers used to stare at him," said Kay, "but down around Yarmouth, everybody knew everyone else and they were used to it so no one thought anything of it. I don't know that it ever bothered him; he took it in stride I guess." (Did Kay intend a pun?) It seems Alphée's mother did *not* take her son's long-footed stride in stride. She didn't want him to make an issue of his difference any more than he did. "Somebody wanted him to go in the circus to make a lot of money," Kay said, "to show his feet in the circus, but he wouldn't go."

Alphée's fourth cousin, 11-year-old Adrien Stuart, holds the bigfoot's really big shoe.

Alphée refused the life of freak shows and big-tops. He could have followed in the large footsteps of two other exceptional Nova Scotians who profited in the previous century from their exceptional appearances: the giantess, Anna Swan, and the Cape Breton giant, Angus MacAskill who both chose to work the circus circuit. Anna and Angus were tall; he was 7 ft. 9 in., she a couple of inches taller. She also surpassed him in her commitment to circus sideshows. Angus didn't stick with it for long. His circus career came up short for a giant. After injuring himself lifting an anchor, he returned to Nova Scotia to live out his days running a general store in Cape Breton.

Anna, however, enjoyed a large measure of success from her measurement of height. Born in 1846 in Central New Annan, near Tatamagouche in Colchester County, Anna Swan spent much of her life on stages around the world. She joined the famous Mr. Barnum's museum show in New York City. When she toured England, she was presented to an amazed—if not amused—Queen Victoria. Anna sailed back to New York by ocean liner where she met another giant, Captain Martin VanBuren Bates. Together they set off to tour Europe. The two giants fell in love during the overseas voyage. They celebrated their wedding in London. Queen Victoria presented Anna with a diamond ring. The huge, happy couple returned to Nova Scotia to

Giantess Anna Swan, Nova Scotia's tallest.

see Anna's family where they were cheered and celebrated. Eventually, they settled south of the border in a comfortable, custom-made house in Ohio.

All of that could have been Alphée Deveau's life. "Live on stage! Never before seen anywhere in the world! The Canadian Bigfoot!" Yes, it might have happened that way. But Alphée wasn't the show-biz type. He was more an Angus than an Anna. He stuck to home perhaps because he had a vow to keep. "I guess he had promised his mother he wouldn't do that," Kay Deveau remarked.

The closest the gentle Alphée Deveau ever came to being a public spectacle was during a trip to the big city. He went to Halifax with his cousin, Henry Deveau's brother, who was tiny in comparison—just under five feet. The long and the short of it was that they made headlines in the next day's *Chronicle-Herald* newspaper. There for the world (at least the local world) to see was the odd couple walking down Halifax's streets, side by side in awkward stride. What a sight. According to Henry Deveau, it made a great photo.

For *Gros Pieds*, Alphée Deveau, that was fame enough. He was neither a showman, a performer, nor a self-promoter, by any stretch—even a size 24. He preferred a quiet life of friends and family, a life of hard work in the woods and mills along the French shore. Perhaps only those close to Alphée knew that his shyness was as deep as his feet were long.

Alphée's niece, Ruth (Deveau) Melanson of the Acadian community of Saulnierville, remembers her uncle well. They were close and Alphée enjoyed being with Ruth's young children. They marvelled over the bulbous toes at the end of those enormous… well, you know. Ruth remembers Alphée as a good man, though at times sad. He worried that he would never find a wife willing to accept his long feet. Alphée's lament came true. He never married.

As Alphée got older he became ill. The nurses at the hospital put a stool at the end of his bed to support his large feet which stuck out over the edge of the bed. Alphée Deveau died on May 23, 1976 at age sixty-eight. His niece, Ruth, makes sure that Alphée's memory is kept alive. She told me that each year she sets up a public display in Alphée's memory at a tourist shop and museum called *La Vieille Maison*, The Old House, in the Acadian community of Meteghan. She places one of Alphée's big, custom-made, black boots beside a photograph of him standing tall in front of the Salmon River Church. Under a grey, brimmed cap and horn-rimmed glasses, his long face bears a shy grin. His big hands are folded humbly together at his belt. He wears a plaid lumberjack shirt and a dark, Sunday-best suit. And yes, at the bottom of the snapshot, his unavoidable, unmistakable big feet. *Les Gros Pieds*.

Clearly, this humble Nova Scotia Bigfoot has left a big imprint—or footprint, if you will—on the memories of those who knew him best.

Giants, Mutants, and Culture

The great two-headed calf debate.

You know, I could regale you with Nova Scotian oddities until the cows come home. And they have. Come home, that is. I'm speaking about the 100-year-old two-headed calves of Tatamagouche. (No, I am not making this up.) The century-old calves stand about as high as your… calves. They have come home to the Sunrise Trail Museum after they were banished to the Fraser cultural centre in downtown Tatamagouche, where they stood, losing hair, for seventeen years. A tantalizing attraction. One calf has two heads up front. That means four eyes, two noses, two mouths and four ears, all at one end. Yuck. At the other end, just one tail. Imagine that.

The other small brown calf is different. It has no tail. Instead, it has a perfectly formed head at each end. "How now, brown cow?" It lived just four days. (I think you can guess why it died.) How oddly fascinating yet strangely repulsive.

Eventually, some of the cultural centre's board members thought these freaks of nature somehow didn't fit in an art gallery of fine watercolours and creative photography. (Go figure.) Yet others thought these genetic moo-tations were a great draw. A debate ensued—taste versus tourism.

Like the calves themselves, the board was of two minds. But I guess they put their heads together and a decision was reached.

The matted-haired calves were kindly accepted back at the nearby Sunrise Trail Museum which originally had tossed them aside for the same reason: they're gross! Nevertheless, the cows came home.

The cultural centre board agreed to keep the eight-foot swan. Anna Swan, that is. The famous 7-ft., 11.5-in. giantess of the Tatamagouche area is commemorated by a display of clothes and photos. She had just one head. On the top.

I guess two-headed cows are no match for eight-foot women. (I never thought I would ever write that). Cows with two heads and giant women. Remind me not to drink the Tatamagouche water.

Morse Code, Mutiny, and Missiles

One Nova Scotian's memories of messaging methods.

"Daddy, why is there a big wooden ship's mast on top of Citadel Hill?" "Because son, that's where the *Bluenose* is buried." (This conversation, between a tourist and his son, was actually overheard by one of our Nova Scotia eavesdroppers.)

As the saying goes, those who don't learn their history are condemned to look stupid. The kid's question, though, is a good one. Dad's answer is creative but wrong. Think about it. Why are there towering ships' masts protruding skyward from the fort on top of a huge mound of earth? Of course it looks silly to the historically uninitiated! No ships up there. Was it some land-locked, frustrated sea captain trying to cope with a posting he hated? Did he live his dreary days "sailing" his fortified hill on the briny ocean of his imagination? No. (But it would make a great story.)

The fact is, those masts and yard-arms represent Nova Scotia's earliest form of communication across the province. Our first attempt to reach out and touch someone. Long before the historic Morse code cable came ashore near Canso. Long before Marconi erected his marvellous towers of wireless communication at Table Head, Cape Breton. Long before Mr. Bell of Baddeck placed his first phone call. Before all those innovations, there was another ingenious messaging experiment conducted in Nova Scotia. It was visual telegraphy—our earliest precursor to the long-distance phone call. Its inventor is unknown, but its builder was none other than Prince Edward, Duke of Kent. I learned about it from a veteran Nova Scotian expert in distance communication.

My informant, a legend in his own time, is a retired radio operator whose passion for the magical innovations of Marconi and Morse took him around the world. He was involved in a classic Hollywood blockbuster motion picture. And he was in the middle of an international political crisis that almost prompted a third world war. We Nova Scotians sure do get around. He even has a movie-hero kind of

He sends signals by the seashore. A young Spud Roscoe flashes messages aboard *Bounty*.

name. Spurgeon G. Roscoe, at your service. He knows of what he speaks. His friends call him "Spud."

Spud Roscoe has been fascinated with through-the-air communication his whole life. He spent his working days sending and receiving transmissions of one sort or another for various employers: the Royal Canadian Navy, Metro Goldwyn Mayer Inc., Department of Transport, Gypsum Transportation Ltd., the Royal Canadian Mounted Police, and the Canadian Coast Guard. Get the message? Spud did. In fact he got thousands and thousands of messages over the years. Using Morse code transmission keys, radio transmitters, and flashing signal lamps, Spud did it all. That's why Spud wouldn't have missed for the world the poignant closing-down ceremony at the Canadian Coast Guard's ship-to-shore radio station at Ketch Harbour, near Halifax, November 19, 1996.

The largest marine radio station in Canada, the Halifax Coast Guard Radio station, call-sign VCS, began in 1905. But it succumbed to the unstoppable spread of a newer, more advanced satellite technology.

After 1999, there will be no more Morse in marine communication. And so, an electronic euthanasia was performed at the historic communication station. A pulling of the plug—literally. A group of grey-haired, retired radio operators gathered to pay their respects on that bleak November day. They had spent their careers listening to the familiar "dah-dah-de-de-dah-dah-de" sound that Morse code operators can decipher in their sleep. It's a beautiful, nostalgic sound. A sound evoking vague visions reaching across vast distances, to exotic and interesting places. It's the sound of a wish and a promise. A whisper in the air. That's why Spud Roscoe was there that day with his fellow operators, to say goodbye to an old friend. One of his older communications comrades was given the honour of pressing the key to send out the last message. It was a straightforward directive to "all ships at sea," letting them know VCS was shutting down ship-to-shore communications for good—or for worse, depending on who you ask. A few courteous replies of good luck and best wishes came from ships within range. Then it was over. The end of an era.

Spud and I stood in that radio room a few days later. It was stripped of equipment. Wires dangled from the ceiling. Bare patches in the carpet showed where desks had been. The building was being downsized. It didn't feel progressive, it felt sad. But there, in that empty room in Ketch Harbour, Spud took me back through the ages of through-the-air communication in Nova Scotia, beginning with the marvel of visual telegraphy in this province, two hundred years ago.

The French were first to develop the messaging system during the Napoleonic wars. Formally adopted in 1792, it is known nowadays as a semaphore system, a signalling using flags and a code. In the land-based system, two stations could communicate, each having an upright post with a crosspiece on which two revolving arms could be fixed in certain positions. Assorted flags would be run up the posts according to the coded message. The hilltop stations needed to be visible by telescope. Some claimed a brief message could be sent 150 miles in fifteen minutes. That's ten miles a minute. (Unlike phone calls today, which cost ten cents a minute—but only at certain times of the week.) The British Admiralty borrowed the semaphore system from the French, then toyed with a

Swedish shutter system of signalling.

During the late 1700s, the Admiralty overseas experimented with one communication system then the next. (Choosing a long distance provider is complicated. If only someone would come out with a flat fee: anyday, anytime, anywhere!) While the Admiralty experimented, an efficient and rapid system of visual telegraphy was devised and installed right here in Nova Scotia.

Thomas H. Raddall, the celebrated Nova Scotian historian wrote about this early "Vis-Tel," shall we call it, in "Nova Scotia's First Telegraph System," *Dalhousie Historical Review*, 1947:

> Its inventor remains unknown but its builder was none other than Prince Edward, Duke of Kent, at that time commanding the forces in Nova Scotia and chiefly known in history as the father of Queen Victoria. For at least two years his telegraph was in active use between Halifax and Annapolis, a distance of about 130 miles and the system was in course of extension around the Bay of Fundy and up the St. John valley of Fredericton when Prince Edward withdrew to England and the scheme fell through. Had he remained in North America, it was his evident intention to continue the line to Quebec and perhaps beyond, where it would have made an important difference to the lonely British struggles in Upper Canada during the War of 1812. But that was not to be.

This prince was particularly committed to making things happen under his command in Nova Scotia. Vis-Tel began at Camperdown, a hill at Portuguese Cove, near Chebucto Head. Thomas Raddall himself was a signal sender at that station. But way back in the visual telegraphy days, a signal could be sent from that hill to be read by men at York Redoubt, then relayed to the Halifax Citadel, which could relay it out along the edge of Bedford Basin. (Prince Edward also had a signal post at his lovenest estate so he could work at home. Seriously. It is documented that he even ordered executions by visual telegraphy. The first home office in Nova Scotia! I wonder if he had voice mail? "I'm sorry, I'm unable to read your signals right now, please leave your message after the red flag, and I'll get back to you.")

The message could be sent further along signal stations, from the Prince's place out to Windsor and across the province, then down to Annapolis Royal. The Prince ordered that trees be cleared all along the way so signal stations could view each other's flags by telescope. Clear-cutting for clearer communication! Each signal station was staffed by the Prince's men and had provisions and signalling equipment. A variety of coloured flags and big, black wicker balls were hoisted on the signal masts in varying order, according to an agreed code. The method was relatively rapid, although there was one particular message that took as long as six hours to make the trip from Halifax to Annapolis Royal. Maybe there wasn't a good wind for flag flying that day. Or perhaps it was too foggy. "I'm sorry, there seems to be a lot of fog on the line. Please hang up and try your call again."

So, that was Vis-Tel, an early Nova Scotian communication system. The closest thing to "chat rooms" in the latter 1700s. I was fascinated by the history that Spud was spouting. But when Spud casually mentioned his first Morse code duty at sea was on board HMS *Bounty* the flags went up. Huh? Was Spud telling me that he was Captain Bligh's radio operator? Should I suggest a twelve-step program— Anachronism Anonymous. Luckily I hid my incredulity. He meant the *movie* version of the *Bounty*. Of course. This *Bounty* was built in Lunenburg for the 1962 Hollywood epic, "Mutiny on the Bounty," with Marlon Brando as Fletcher Christian and Trevor Howard as Captain Bligh. A great flick. And a true story. The movie tells the tale of the crew's mutiny off Tahiti in 1789, a few years before the Nova Scotia experiment with Vis-Tel. Several Nova Scotians were part of the *Bounty* replica's crew hired by Metro Goldwyn Mayer. Spurgeon G. Roscoe signed on as the Morse code operator on board.

This replica of the eighteenth-century vessel was not just a movie set. It actually had to float *and* sail. *Bounty* set course for Tahiti to shoot the big mutiny scene. Spud's job was to transmit and receive messages between MGM and the good ship *Bounty*. He received weather reports and sent the ship's location and other information to the movie makers back home. Now anyone who has seen the movie must remember the island paradise scene. There were lots of scantily-clad Tahitian swimmers. Spud remembers that Marlon Brando was always delaying the shooting by going for a swim with the island girls, and the director would have to wait for Brando's hair to dry for the next scene. Spud had to be in costume too, in case the camera caught him in the background.

"We had to grow our hair long and wear a striped T-shirt and buckled shoes and everything," said Spud. "And we had to make sure we didn't have our wedding rings on, or a wristwatch or eyeglasses. In case the camera caught us." The movie magicians were quite anti-anachronistic, even without a twelve-step program. But there is one anomaly that always catches his eye whenever he sees a picture of *Bounty* in the local video store or on late night TV.

"I can always tell it's my *Bounty*," Spud said proudly, "because I can see my antenna." His *radio's* antenna that is. But who knows? Maybe all those years of radio transmitting had—literally—gone to his head. Just to be safe, I asked him to describe its location.

"It looks like a piece of the rigging. We had a small RCA radar. We had the antenna, the scanner, for the radio in the foremast. You'd see it every time you saw the ship. I can point it out to you. It's the white insulator at the top of the mizen-mast and runs down the side. There's one scene where Trevor Howard and Marlon Brando are getting into it, and I can see the antenna running down behind them, into the radio room." Cool! Marconi on the *Bounty*. Spud's contribution to the movie business, long before it was common for Nova Scotians, was recorded forever in history. Sure, it was just a wire, but it was Spud's wire.

Lunenburgers built the ship. But Spud was responsible for that wire. Spud Roscoe's involvement in the movie wasn't all below-deck messaging. Once he had to help out Captain Bligh when he took on too much liquid cargo, and started to list. Trevor Howard lost his "sea legs." You could say he was out of character. Spud had to help a staggering Howard back on board *Bounty* while a huge crowd watched from the dock. Oh, the glamour of moviemaking in a tropical paradise. Later, Spud was immersed in global political crisis, while sailing home from Tahiti. It was October, 1962. Spud loves to tell what happened next:

"We were just off of Cuba when Kennedy decided to pull his Cuban missile crisis there and then. That kept me pretty busy that night, I'll tell you. I was up on the deck all evening on the signal light and when these aircraft would spot us on radar, they'd come down out of nowhere! And when they came on top of us they'd switch on their landing lights. There was no VHF radio in those days, so I'd just flash, on the signal light, the name of the vessel, "the *Bounty*"! Ha! Ha! I can almost hear those guys in the aircraft saying, 'How long has this ship been out here anyway?'"

Lucky for Spud, those protective pilots understood Morse code. Modern satellite imaging wouldn't have helped *Bounty* get out of that fix. Spud's constant messaging saved the ship and crew in the midst of a very tense political stand off. John F. Kennedy, of course, had ordered Russian ships transporting the missiles to Cuba to turn back or face the consequences. *Bounty* had to be careful she wasn't blown out of the water by a nervous pilot tracking Russian missiles.

"They'd do two or three circles and look us over before they'd take off, but not one of them put a signal lamp in the aircraft widow to have a chat with me. I was all alone on the Morse code end of it." Imagine! Spud Roscoe standing in the dark on the deck of that tiny ship bobbing on the black surface of the immense Atlantic ocean. Missile loaded Soviet ships close at hand, armed military planes circling overhead. The Americans and Russians were playing chicken with nuclear weapons and Spud was in the middle of it. And he just stood there in the cold, flashing.

He could even hear the Russian ship's transmission. Their radio operators were feeling very nervous. Spud was nervous too. Would the American fighters take him seriously? Would they remember the old axiom not to shoot the messenger? Spud tried to be convincing. "Yes, this is HMS *Bounty*, and no, you are not two hundred years off course!" Fortunately, the incident blew over instead of blowing up. The floating anachronism reached the American coastline safely and immediately went on tour, promoting the movie and greeting huge crowds of fans at every port.

Morse code, mutiny, and missiles. What's to be learned from this strange confluence of historical events? Well, I guess it's not only true that history *repeats* itself; sometimes history *meets* itself.

Nova Scotia's *Bounty* in paradise—an MGM promotional photo.

Lights, Camera, Lobster!
How Nova Scotia made Liz Taylor cry.

I dream of Genie. The Genie with the heart-shaped head and single gold leg. Genie is the award presented to great Canadian film makers. We've been making films for a long time. In fact, Canada's proud film-making heritage began in, you guessed it, Nova Scotia. Surprise, surprise. Isn't this where all good things begin? Yes, we were first to produce a feature-length film. And it was based on a feature-length poem, Longfellow's *Evangeline*.

The 1847 romantic epic was made into a movie by the Canadian Bioscope Company in 1913. But romance became a mystery. The movie disappeared. A film history expert in Halifax, Ron Foley Macdonald, told me that the only remaining evidence of that first flick is a few cast photos and paper advertisements. "It's like the Holy Grail," said Ron, "People are looking for it everywhere."

The Canadian Bioscope Company was shot down economically in the First World War, when the bomb-makers confiscated the nitrate used in making film. Yet newsreels were still produced so folks would be informed. Like the bomb-makers, makers of newsreels did a booming business for a while. Then in 1918, the Ford Motor Company shot a promotional film of North End Halifax recovering from the great explosion. Ford's questionable marketing plan was to encourage car sales by promoting interesting places to visit. "Come on kids, pile in, let's drive to see devastation in Nova Scotia!"

It was no accident that Canadian place names also started showing up in Hollywood movie scripts! This in*genie*ious marketing agreement between our government and the movie makers was negotiated by Prime Minister Mackenzie King. He thought it would have a subliminal effect on tourists. "Come on kids, pile in, let's drive to Nova Scotia." "Why?" "Ahh, I'm not sure... "

Sad to say, it didn't work on Elizabeth Taylor. She sobbed bitterly when she learned she'd have to come to Nova Scotia. In the original 1950 version of *Father of the Bride*, Taylor's character weeps openly to her father (played by Spencer Tracy) about the honeymoon plans her groom is foisting upon her. "Nova Scotia for a honeymoon," she bawls, "it can't be Nova Scotia... so he can fish some horrible salmon or something. I told him I wanted to go someplace romantic but he said there was nothing as romantic as a fishing shack in Nova Scotia! (sniff!)"

Unfaithfully Yours, 1948, was kinder and gentler. It mentioned without malice the town of Antigonish.

Eventually Hollywood producers themselves found good reason to come here, despite Elizabeth Taylor's teary tantrum. To heck with Liz, I agree with Spencer Tracy. Our fishing shacks *are* romantic. We like them, we *really* like them!

Dead Man Waking

Eye to eye with the ghost of Prince's Lodge.

Boo! Now, that's no way to begin a ghost story. Too cute. Too cliché. The old tale of the ghost of Prince's Lodge in Halifax is anything but cute. But it is cliché. A wronged spirit forever haunts his place of death in search of justice! Been there, done that, bought the big white sheet, and cut out the eyeholes. But the cliché crumbles when you are given a clear, detailed description of the ghost from a credible eyewitness. Instantly, two hundred years of spooky folklore is brought to life by the trembling voice of one man; a man who hadn't spoken publicly about the apparition for over twenty-five years… until he spoke to me.

It's true. I was the envy of my journalistic peers. By unearthing a fresh angle I managed to get an exclusive on this well-buried Nova Scotia spook story. The story is two centuries old. Luckily my specialty is retroactive journalism. Everything old can become new again.

Pursuant to the protocol of Nova Scotia Know-It-All-ism, my search began, as usual, with a request from a CBC Radio listener. Elizabeth Howell, of Halifax, phoned the radio station to say she wanted to know more about the ghost of Prince's Lodge. She said she found no reference to it in *Bluenose Ghosts*—the revered collection of Nova Scotia spirit stories compiled by our patron saint of folklore, the late Helen Creighton. Leaving the book aside, I set forth to make my own mark in ghost storydom. I was Helen Creighton with a beard and a better tape recorder! Helen would be proud. The mission was successful, thanks again to a little research and a touch of good luck that seems to haunt such Nova Scotian investigations.

First, the background to this story: The Prince's Lodge refers to an area between the Halifax peninsula and the community of Bedford. It overlooks the beautiful Bedford Basin (which is hard to overlook, by the way). It's pretty wide and deep. Visualize Halifax Harbour as the shape of a keyhole—the basin forms the rounded end.

In the 1790s, Queen Victoria's father, who was then Prince Edward, Duke of Kent, built an extravagant mansion on this sloping, waterfront acreage. He added a pleasure garden including beautiful trails and a pond. There were barracks for his soldiers and down near the water's edge, a lovely rotunda, for the enjoyment of his lady-love, Alphonsine Thérèse Bernadine Julie de Montgenet de Saint Laurent, Baronne de Fortisson, Madame Saint Laurent. Just so we don't strain ourselves, let's call her Julie.

The serenity of Julie's idyllic waterside retreat was shattered one early July morning by the sound of clanging. A deadly duel was in progress. The duel is described in a book by William Borrett who once lived on the Prince's Lodge grounds. In 1948 he published a collection of historical Nova Scotia stories which he had first told on CHNS Radio in Halifax. (A lazy practice of selling recycled radio research in book form for a few extra bucks. I hate that!)

According to Borrett, the Prince and his mistress threw a lavish reception at Prince's Lodge. The food and drink flowed like an overly flowery, creatively ambitious, but clumsily executed run-on sentence.

Some drank too much and probably spoke in run-on sentences. Somebody said something he shouldn't have. Among the guests was Colonel Olgilvie, an accomplished swordsman whose blade had recently killed an opponent in England.

A heated argument broke out betwixt the colonel and a Captain Howard. A duel was arranged. The two met at dawn, just south of the rotunda. Both men died of their wounds. Not a nice way to end a late party. In Halifax today it would be more likely to end with donairs. Anyway, Prince Edward was furious. He ordered the colonel's slashed body to be buried where he fell, without the proper protocol of military honours.

According to folklore, the dead colonel's ghost was occasionally seen wandering the Prince's Lodge grounds seeking a respectable burial. According to Borrett, the last sighting was in 1888.

But I learned that there was an unreported sighting in 1972. Fred Desjardins, then a nineteen-year-old university student living with his parents near the rotunda, awoke at two o'clock one morning to see a ghost dressed in military uniform at the foot of his bed. Today, Fred is a writer though ghost stories aren't his genre.

The rotunda is known as "the Round House." It's perched atop a knoll, jammed between Bedford Basin and the railway tracks alongside busy Bedford Highway.

Today, the domed roof of the small, round, white wooden building is crowned with a big, white wooden ball. The inside is the size of the average one-bedroom apartment, sans corners.

The Round House of Prince's Lodge: a ghostly haunt for a long-dead soldier.

To provide atmosphere to our interview, I arranged to take Fred inside the round house and down the creaky stairs, into the musty, stone-walled cellar.

The perfect spot, I thought, for Fred Desjardins to tell his story. Here he was, on the ghost's turf, to describe for the first time in twenty-five years the strange apparition he had seen in 1972.

Fred couldn't explain why he awoke early that morning. He just did. In the darkness, he saw a strange mass taking the shape of a human figure. Dead man waking.

"Suddenly," Fred explained, "this… mass started to develop a human-like form. It also developed a brilliant radiance. Everything else in the room was very dim and dark, but this particular figure was glowing brightly, as though you were looking at it in bright sunshine." Okay; so there's a shiny man in a dark room. That's odd enough in itself, but there's more. This shiny man looked like an eighteenth-century British soldier. His hair and mustache were long. He wore a dark cloak. He was reaching for his sword, and he was angry!

"He had his hand on a sword handle protruding from the front of the cloak, and he had the most intensely angry look I have ever seen on a person's face. He was glowering directly into my eyes."

Fred's a writer so his choice of "glowering" was no accident.

Sitting in the spooky cellar of the old round house, Fred described what happened next.

"I'm not a particularly brave person and I am astonished that I simply didn't rush right out of the room in terror." No kidding. For a moment, Fred couldn't move. Paralysis has that effect. But what he did next defies explanation.

"I inched my way closer and closer to the apparition, which was opaque but almost as solid as a human being. I crawled closer until I was virtually nose to nose with the thing. By this point my mind was screaming, 'This is not going away. He looked as though he wanted to kill me.'" Fred chuckled nervously. I could tell by the fear in his eyes and his heavy breathing that he was reliving the story. "What's it like to stare a live dead man dead in the face?" I asked.

"It was the greatest sense of fatalism I've ever had. This thing not only looked as though he wanted to kill me he looked like he was going to. It was like being before a firing squad… just apoplectic. But I suddenly became bizarrely calm."

Fred's calmness agitated me. The good thing about ghost stories is that they make you scared. "What happened next?" I asked, hoping for the worst.

"He suddenly withdrew," said Fred "Very much like you'd see in a B-movie. He simply wisped off into nothing with a 'whooshing' sound." Darn. The cellar was warm but I felt chilled. Wait a minute. Something's missing. Did Fred have prior knowledge of what this ghost looked like? Was his imaginative, young mind simply replaying a local ghost story from memory? No. Fred insisted he hadn't known anything about the soldier's ghost until he saw it that night in his room. I believe him.

In 1972, shortly after the event, Fred had confided the story of his ghostly encounter to his close friend and neighbour, Scott Murray who was living in the Round House with his mother at the time.

Fred told me that Scott's mother, Nonnie, immediately recognized Fred's description of the ghost and showed Fred an old book that described other sightings of a ghostly soldier wrapped in a military cloak. Fred's early-morning eyewitness spirit-sighting was corroborated.

I had the feeling that there was certainly more to this story than meets the eye. It was nothing to boo at. Even the way I had found Fred in the first place was strange.

When I first got wind of the ghost of the Round House, I made some fumbling phone calls which led me to Scott Murray, the one-time occupant of Prince's Lodge Round House and now a doctor in Halifax. He told me he had never cornered a ghost in his circular home. Never even caught a glimpse of one. But Dr. Murray found it interesting that I had called just days after his old friend Fred Desjardins had contacted him for the first time in more than twenty years. Fred called Scott about some medically-related research he was doing. The two men began reminiscing. Fred confided to Dr. Murray that, for some reason, he had been dwelling recently on the apparition he had witnessed so long ago. Just a week before I called, Fred had told Dr. Murray that it might finally be time for him to speak publicly about what he had seen.

So that's how I became the vehicle for Fred's haunting memory. Was it just lucky timing? Or did the dead colonel need to make his woeful two-hundred-year-old tale known in the 1990s, and used Fred and myself as his mediums? The ghost didn't want his story to die too.

Maybe the coincidence of my call was no coincidence at all.

The Christmas Ghost

The haunting of Nova Scotia's first Christmas tree.

Glittering, graceful, sparkling, symbolic, nostalgic, lovely and green, a Christmas tree warms the hardest heart. The old Yule–tide tree tradition in Canada began right here in Nova Scotia. The first decorated, indoor tree was erected in an old house in our provincial capital. The house at 6454 Coburg Road in Halifax was built about 1815. Known as Coburg Cottage, it has three levels of small rooms with low ceilings. In 1846, William Pryor brought this first tree across the threshold to honour the custom of his wife's homeland—Germany. I still utter an annual clenched-jaw "thank you" to dear Mr. Pryor while vacuuming those ubiquitous spruce needles from my carpet. God Bless them, every one. Trevor and Justine Housser now live in the old Pryor

Our first Christmas Tree as shown on the Housser Family Christmas card.

home. They offered me a tour of the house and one of their special Christmas cards. A sketch of the old house shows Mr. Pryor carrying the first tree to the door. But with the tree came a ghost—a Christmas presence. The Housser's grown daughter, Debbie, lives in the tiny, upper rooms. She remembers, years ago, seeing mysterious red lights floating above her bed at night… a sudden breeze blowing the tinsel on her own tiny attic tree, though all of the windows were shut tightly.

"Then I would wake up hearing what I thought was the cry of a baby," Debbie told me calmly. She decided to investigate this ghost of Christmas past.

"I went to the archives and found that Mrs. Pryor's infant child had died of unknown circumstances on the third floor where I was sleeping." Debbie was not shaken though. She found the ghost somehow comforting. And at Christmas time, the spirit of an infant child seems somehow appropriate, doesn't it? Especially in the home of our very first Christmas tree.

The Little Town That Wouldn't

Nova Scotian workers unite in two troubled towns.

Labour strife. A tough, steel-plant town. Miners fighting for their rights. It sounds like a scenario from Cape Breton's history. It's not; I'm referring to the mainland community of Londonderry, near Truro in Colchester County between Great Village and Folly Lake. Today it's a quiet village, but in 1877 it was a bustling boom town of about 5,000, called Acadia Mines. A renowned scientist and inventor, Dr. Carl W. Siemens, was a key player in the town's success. Siemens had devised a faster way to process iron ore into steel and built a steel plant in Acadia Mines to test his new method. It was a two million-dollar investment— a lot of money back then! About as much as the government gives Sysco each week.

Acadia Mines flourished. So thankful was the provincial government to Dr. Siemens that they enacted a law that officially renamed the town Siemens. (Dr. Siemens' swanky VIP parties on his private boat in Halifax Harbour probably had no bearing on the politicians' decision.)

But to Siemens' (the company, that is) chagrin, the new town name didn't stick. A spokesman for the company wondered during an interview with me, "What would happen if a province enacted a law and nobody followed it?"

Oops! It's true. No one accepted the town's new name. Not the citizens. Not the Post Office. No one. So it remained "Acadia Mines" until the Londonderry Iron and Mining Company gave the town its present name in 1903.

The present-day Siemens Electric Ltd. couldn't find old Nova Scotia maps with the name Siemens on it. They ran advertisements in Nova Scotia newspapers asking for leads, but no one responded.

Trueman Matheson, a Londonderry historian, thinks he knows why the townspeople of long ago ignored the name change that honoured their chief employer: DWS—old fashioned Downtrodden-Workers Syndrome—a traditional Nova Scotian affliction.

Trueman told me the iron-ore miners went on strike when the company decreased their pay cheques. Replacement workers were brought in. A riot broke out. A company man was beaten. Stop me if you've heard this before.

The company brought in troops by train from Halifax. A miner was shot dead. Sound familiar? Cape Bretoners still remember the tragic story of William Davis, who was killed in the street by company troops. After the Acadia Mines riot, miners faced charges. As in the William Davis incident, the company got away with murder, literally.

So, what's in a name? Plenty of resentment, it sounds like. And a whole lot of worker solidarity.

Not so Simple Simon, the Sky Man

The genius astronomer who brought order to the universe.

When I heard the learn'd astronomer,
When the proofs, the figures, were ranged in columns before me,
When I was shown the charts and diagrams, to add, divide,
    and measure them,
When I sitting heard the astronomer where he lectured with much
    applause in the lecture room,
How soon unaccountable I became tired and sick,
Till rising and gliding out I wander'd off by myself,
In the mystical moist night-air, and from time to time,
Look'd up in perfect silence at the stars.

    Walt Whitman
    When I Heard the Learn'd Astronomer

Long lectures make me tired and sick too.
    Bruce Nunn
    Mr. Nova Scotia Know-it-All

Here's a question for you: What do Walt Whitman, Albert Einstein, President James Garfield, and Sherlock Holmes have in common? I know that sounds like a Harvard professor's lame joke, but the question is key to this story.

Even in humour, who would ever see a connection between those sundry figures from history? I would. But it's no joke. The answer is that one Nova Scotian influenced them all, while making a huge name for himself as a world-respected astronomer and economist who dabbled in psychic research. By "influenced" I mean that he helped

Albert Einstein develop the theory of relativity, he inspired Walt Whitman's poetry, and he worked on an invention to save a critically wounded American president. He is even credited with inspiring Sir Arthur Conan Doyle's famous Sherlock Holmes stories.

Not bad for a day's work.

Actually, all of this happened over the chock-full life span of our scientific hero, Simon Newcomb.

I first heard of Newcomb when a mathematician in Halifax, Dr. Karl Dilcher, wrote to me via the CBC e-mail address asking if I had ever heard of "Simon Newcomb's Problem." I thought that his question sounded rather personal, but I'd look into it. Dr. Dilcher had read about Simon Newcomb and his problem in a magazine; the article mentioned that Newcomb was actually born and raised in Nova Scotia. Dr. Dilcher wanted to learn more. I was on the case.

I learned that Simon Newcomb was born on March 12, 1835, in Wallace Bridge, on the beautiful Northumberland shore of Cumberland County.

As for Newcomb's Problem, it was neither personal nor private. It's a hypothetical brainteaser also

Nova Scotia's Simon Newcomb: he saw that the universe was unfolding as it should.

known as Newcomb's Paradox. A conundrum. A dilemma. Newcomb's Paradox is a far cry from the great scientific contributions made by this genius astronomer. In fact, his greatest contribution to the world was *out* of this world—he put the heavens in order.

Simon Newcomb completely standardized the means of computing lunar and planetary tables. In the latter 1800s, there was a lot of variation in the way scientists calculated the movements of planets and moons. Newcomb reduced it all to mathematical order thus creating an international standard used by astronomers until computers came along.

Because of Simon Newcomb's brilliant sky schedule scientists were able to know, for example, the exact timing of the total eclipse of the sun in 1972. Nova Scotia was a popular vantage point for spectators to watch the remarkable display.

One such spectator was the wealthy industrialist, Cyrus Eaton (the man behind the famous Pugwash Thinkers Conference). In chairs set up on his back lawn in Pugwash, Nova Scotia, Eaton awaited the eclipse with his guest, the famous astronomer, Carl Sagan. The two men watched as the moon began to cover the sun. They were sitting just a few miles from Wallace Bridge where Simon Newcomb had been born 137 years earlier. Talk about a small world… in a well-ordered universe.

It was in Wallace Bridge that Simon Newcomb's knowledge of the universe began unfolding at a very young age.

Newcomb says in his 1903 autobiography, *Reminiscences of an Astronomer*, that he knew the alphabet by age four. His father, John Burton Newcomb, a poor school teacher, encouraged Simon to read about astronomy from a young age.

Simon's first scientific experiment was conducted on a neighbouring Nova Scotia farmer. Young Simon secretly removed the tobacco from the farmer's pipe one evening and replaced it with a much cheaper but similarly coloured substance.

The farmer puffed away nonchalantly while Simon observed from a nearby hiding place. The farmer continued to smoke the pipe, commenting only that the tobacco wasn't exactly his cup of tea. In fact, it was. Newcomb had stuffed the pipe with tea leaves.

Unfortunately, at just seven years old, Newcomb lost his humour and his will. He had a mental breakdown. He withdrew from all boyish activity. His father writes in his journal that when young Simon finally emerged from his dark state he had to re-learn the advanced math skills he'd had before his deep depression. (Surely a fast route to a relapse!) Nevertheless, Simon recovered fully. He did not, however, attend school regularly after that—unless you count attending Harvard, *summa cum laude!* Obviously, one or two things had changed somewhere between Simon's depression and Harvard's highest honours.

In search of a teaching job, Simon's father moved the family to Clementsport, Nova Scotia. Shortly after, Newcomb's mother died at the young age of thirty-seven. A teenage Simon decided to strike out on his own. He crossed the Bay of Fundy in a small boat and walked north to Moncton, New Brunswick where he stayed with his maternal grandfather, "Squire" Thomas Prince. In Moncton, Simon was apprenticed to Dr. Foshay, an eccentric herbalist who worked him hard and taught him little. Simon left a note and set out, again on foot, to walk south to the United States. He liked to walk.

Simon worked his way down the coast, then worked his way up the ladder—the professional academic ladder. In the early days of the American Civil War, Simon became professor of mathematics at the US Naval Observatory in Washington. He conducted astronomical observations there for thirty-six years and became a central figure in the most important scientific organizations. He taught mathematics and astronomy at Johns Hopkins University, edited the *American Journal of Mathematics*, and headed up the American Astronomical Society. Simon received many prestigious awards and wrote close to five hundred publications. He was recognized as one of the greatest astronomers of the nineteenth century.

Not bad for a grade school dropout.

Albert Einstein was certainly impressed. That's because, our not-so-simple Simon from little Wallace Bridge, Nova Scotia, gave Einstein the evidence he needed to prove his ingenious theory of relativity. Simon's calculations had uncovered an unusual anomaly in the planet Mercury's orbit. This was the proof Einstein needed and he "pounced on it." At least that's how science historian, Dr. Albert Moyer described it to me. Dr. Moyer teaches at Virginia Technical University in the Untied Tastes of Camera I—Sorry, my Anagrams are acting up again—he teaches in the United States of America.

"This anomaly was crucial in Albert Einstein's general theory of relativity," Dr. Moyer explained. "It took Einstein's theory of relativity to make sense of that irregularity in the orbit." Wow! That's not a bad accomplishment for a lad from rural Nova Scotia where the "theory of relativity" usually begins with, "What's your father's name?"

Simon Newcomb was such a smart cookie that H. G. Wells' classic tale, *The Time Machine*, refers to Simon Newcomb's four-dimensional geometry. Let's face it, you need a fourth dimension if you plan to travel through time. At least that's what Wells' time travelling character argues in the first chapter of the classic science fiction story. According to the "Traveller," some philosophical people had been asking why we settle for *three* dimensions only—why not another dimension at right angles to the other three? The "Traveller" noted that a Dr. Newcomb had been expounding this theory to the New York Mathematical Society only a month earlier. Okay, so now you know the scientific basis for time travel, thanks to our Simon. So it's odd that while Simon could imagine a fourth dimension suitable for time travel, he couldn't swallow the concept of air travel! Maybe that's because his foot was in the way.

You see, in 1902 Simon allegedly said, "Flight by machines heavier than air is impractical and insignificant if not utterly impossible." Eighteen months later, the Wright brothers got off the ground. Oh well, they were Wright, Simon wasn't. His forecasting skills were clearly lacking. That may help to explain why he later became an economist, founding the American Economic Association.

Now, what about Simon Newcomb as the evil genius criminal? Why not? I've already called him an economist. Actually, it was Sir Arthur Conan Doyle, the brilliant Scottish mystery writer, who portrayed our beloved Simon in this light. One literary theorist says that Doyle created Sherlock Holmes' arch nemesis, Professor Moriarty, in the likeness of our own Professor Newcomb. The literary theorist who draws parallels between Newcomb and the fictional Moriarty is an American astronomer, Bradley Schaefer. Schaefer says that both Newcomb and Moriarty were mathematical geniuses, both wrote treatises on the binomial theorem while in their twenties (who hasn't?), both published papers on the dynamics of asteroids in the 1860s and both worked at small universities. Aha! Elementary!

In fact, Schaefer says Doyle modelled another of his fictional characters —Colonel Moran—after his astronomer friend, Drayson. Elementary my dear reader. Doyle was so unimaginative he based his literary characters on his interesting friends! Hey, I've been there. I've wrestled with the unforgiving blank page. I can forgive such desperate measures. But there's one more clue that clinches the case.

Bradley Schaefer apparently uncovered long excerpts copied from the Sherlock Holmes detective stories written in the hand of Mrs. Simon Newcomb. Yes, he did have a wife, Caroline. She was obviously proud that her husband was used as the prototype for the criminal mastermind, Professor Moriarty—the only man smart enough to outwit Sherlock Holmes. Cumberland County should be proud too.

Other literary-minded types say American poet Walt Whitman was also inspired to write a short poem about our astounding astronomer, Simon Newcomb. Well, actually, "inspired" may be too kind a word. In the poem, *When I Heard the Learn'd Astronomer*, Whitman writes of becoming "tired and sick" while listening to one of Simon's astronomy lectures and walks out to get some fresh air. We've all been there too.

Simon's lectures may have been boring to poets, but he had his exciting moments. One of the most dramatic moments in Simon's life was when he played inventive paramedic to a dying US president. In July 1881, President James Garfield was shot by an assassin. He lay in his bed for more than two months, sweating from the pain of his bullet compounded by the intense Washington summer heat. The White House didn't yet have air conditioning. That's where Simon's inventive mind came in to play.

A friend of Garfield's, Simon offered to try cooling the bedroom of the sweaty, suffering president. Simon later wrote about finding an apparatus in the basement that was designed to cool the air of dairies and apartments. It was a metal box, two or three feet square and some five feet long. Cloths were suspended in a row in the box, catching the cold water from blocks of ice placed on a rack above. Air blown through the box was cooled by contact with the cold, wet cloths. The large device was supposed to lower the temperature of a room. Simon tested it and observed that it simply didn't work. Maybe that's why it was in the basement; waiting for a White House yard sale perhaps?

Simon correctly hypothesized that the forced air needed to be in closer contact with the ice itself. He set up the device to blow air over a case of ice as long as an ordinary room. Tubes were constructed, which carried the cooled air to the ailing President's bedchamber. How about that? Simon invented a way to cut through a politician's hot air.

President Garfield was cooler but still dying. The surgeons— including Dr. Woodward, a pioneer in microphotography— said they could save Garfield's life if they could find the metal musket ball imbedded in the president's body. Simon to the rescue again!

Our hero decided that the best way to locate the buried bullet would be to construct a crude electromagnetic metal detector using a small metal bar wrapped with an electrified wire. He soon realized that the device would not be sensitive enough. He consulted another inventor with a strong Nova Scotia connection—Alexander Graham Bell. Bell devised a telephonic device (of course) to amplify the electromagnetic waves. Simon writes in his autobiography that Bell's device pointed to the location that the surgeons had already pinpointed. However, it turned out that doctors and Bell were mistaken and President Garfield died. An autopsy of Garfield confirmed that Bell's telephonic device was off its mark. Sorry, wrong number.

Why didn't it work? A theory proposed by R. J. Brown, the Editor in Chief of the Newspapers Collectors' Society of America suggests that neither Bell nor Newcomb would have been aware of a new invention that only the wealthy would have in their bedrooms. Brown suggests that Garfield was lying on metal-coil bedsprings; good for a comfy sleep but guaranteed to throw off the metal detector.

Oh well Simon, your air conditioner was probably a big hit. As far as I can tell, Simon's life was full of big hits, until, in July 1909, he died. He had begun life on a lowly Nova Scotia farm and had ascended to high learning, high office, and the high heavens! The complexity of Simon's calculating mind carried him far further than one might think his humble roots would allow. Indeed, it may have been those very roots that brought Simon's genius to the fore. Maybe that's why he returned to Nova Scotia many times over the years, to visit his cousins and the birthplace that propelled him to such great things. I'd like to think that.

Now I know this may seem like the perfect spot to end this story. But we haven't got to Newcomb's problem. Well, a word of warning; It's the kind of frustrating brain-twister that may leave you curled in a corner mumbling and counting your fingers.

Here goes.

Newcomb's Paradox: you agree to take part in an unusual test of a psychic's powers. In front of you are two boxes, A and B. Box A contains a thousand dollar bill. Box B contains either a million dollars or nothing. You cannot see inside the boxes. You must choose to take either box B only, or both boxes. Those are the only options. The catch is that the psychic predicts in advance which box you will choose. The psychic is right 80 per cent of the time. If she predicts that you will take both boxes she will leave box B empty. If she predicts that you will take only box B, she will leave the million dollars in it. What should you do, take both boxes or just box B? Think about it.

Not-so-simple Simon must have died smiling, leaving us with *that* one.

Streets of Gold

Road gold in a Nova Scotian village.

The people of tiny Goldboro, Guysborough County, are fond of saying their roads are paved with gold.

Now they've got gas.

Natural gas is coming ashore to the once bustling but now quiet, gold-mining village. A ceremonial sod-turning was held in that century-old community in January 1998.

Daley Henderson would have been glad to watch. Two years earlier, the aging and amiable sage of Goldboro explained to me that there really is gold in them there roads. As a boy, he used to scavenge for glitter amid the gravel. Later he laboured in a mine that produced the gold.

Daley explained that truckloads of sparkling waste rock from the mines were used to give the Midas touch to his town's travelways.

Streets of gold! *Ripley's Believe It Or Not!* had fun reporting that one.

I'm sad to say that Daley has passed on. He wasn't present for the symbolic sod ceremony. However, Daley's good friend Ken MacLeod was there. Ken tells me that his nephew, Kenny, also picked up gold bits from the road just as Daley did years ago. In fact, Kenny Giffin has a ring his grandfather made from road gold. Now a mechanical engineering technologist, Kenny has a foot in the town's two great industries— the gold boom and the gas (soon).

A native of Goldboro, Kenny also worked in the mines. Now the Sable gas giants are tapping his local expertise to map locations of old, defunct gold mines. They don't want to stake a claim, but rather, to claim their stakes after they mark the land route to lay their gas pipeline. Digging into an abandoned mine shaft would not be good for business.

Kenny told me there were fourteen mines producing gold in his hometown between 1862 and the 1940s. That's a lot of shafts. Combined, they once produced 180 tons per day. But alas, it wasn't all gold. Much of it was rock. Extraction methods were crude. Getting to the glitter was no easy matter. About 40 per cent of the valuable gold deposits were left embedded in the waste rock. One Goldboro mine dumped its wealthy waste, not on the road, but into the harbour. Can prospectors swim?

It doesn't matter because the tiny community has a new prospect. Goldboro, may your gas be as good as gold.

Who Put the "Peggy" in Peggy's Cove?

The definitive story behind the name.

I like Peggy's Cove. I make a Peggy's pilgrimage every year. However, until recently I felt a psychological barrier that made it hard for me to fully appreciate the cove's beauty—the smooth, rounded rocks and crashing waves; the gleaming, white lighthouse with its emerald eye. Proud, pretty Peggy's Cove. It's difficult to truly appreciate the scene without plagiarizing the foggy images of a familiar postcard. The writer, Walker Percy, wrote that the only way to truly emotionally absorb the beauty of

Peggy's Cove light. (Sounds like a new Maritime ale!)

a particular site is to come to it from an altered perspective. See it from a different angle.

Well, lucky me, I've found an angle that lets me appreciate Peggy's place—those cliché photos of the waves breaking before the majestic lighthouse are no longer touristy tripe for me.

My journey to this new level of cove-awareness began one day when I received a tip from a CBC Radio listener, Cynthia Driskill. Rumour had it that a woman claiming to be a direct descendant of the original Peggy was visiting the area. Stop the presses! (Or at least the airwaves.) Could this be the key to discovering the truth behind the folklore?

A genuine germ of fact amid a myriad of sappy, romantic tourist propaganda. A missing link restored in the chain of Nova Scotian history.

The drive out to the cove on a warm September Saturday allowed me time to reflect on this key icon of our provincial character. The wheels in my head turned with the wheels of my car. I drove and I thought. I recalled a friend arguing once that there were numerous local seaside nooks prettier than Peggy's. Maybe so.

Margaret (Peggy) Weaver, who gave her name to our most famous cove.

And yet Peggy's Cove is known around the world. Some tourists have been known to ask if it is our province's capital. It's featured on promotional material and bric-a-brac everywhere. About 700,000 people each year walk the granite rocks and many of them are us! The cove is loved, near and far and the little shop of Peggy paraphernalia does a booming business. The sea sells by the sea, sure.

But what, I mused, did I really know about the history of the name behind Peggy's Cove? The published version available at the cove's gift store was written by a local artist, William Edward deGarthe, who also carved the popular Fisherman's Memorial in the centre of the village.

DeGarthe's account begins with the story of a schooner which was wrecked on Halibut Rock, off the lighthouse point on a stormy October night. The ship ran hard aground and the high waves forced some of her crew to climb the masts. But the waves proved to be too much and everyone on board was washed into the sea forever. Everyone, that is, except a child who was washed ashore where she was found by the locals. The child was given the name Margaret, and she eventually married one of the sons of the

Margaret and Dennis Miller. Her great-grandmother was Peggy of Peggy's Cove.

family who took her in. The story of Peggy's survival spread and people from surrounding areas used to come and visit Peggy of the cove. Before long the village came to be known as Peggy's Cove.

Sounds plausible. William deGarthe relates a second theory as well. Because the cove is situated in St. Margaret's Bay, he suggests that the cove's name may have come from the short form for Margaret. But such an irreverent shortening of a saintly title seems unlikely. It turns out that my roadtrip would confirm deGarthe's first version of events.

Finally I reached my destination, the Teddy Bear Bed and Breakfast in Tantallon, close to the cove where I met the great-granddaughter of the Peggy who was washed ashore in the mid-1800s. Amid the frilly

Teddy Bear decor sat a small woman in her mid-seventies, with short grey hair and big-framed glasses. And yes, her name was Margaret though she is known by her middle name, Maxine. Born Margaret Miller, Maxine later married and became Maxine Roeper. Dennis Roeper shook my hand.

Maxine and her eighty-year-old husband had driven from their home in California to see the sea from Peggy's Cove for the first time. Maxine told me in her slight western-American accent that she used to be a pre-school teacher before she had her own children. She had been curious about Peggy's Cove ever since she was told a dramatic story as a child. A story that had been passed on in her family for two generations.

"From the time I was a little girl," Maxine began, "I have heard of Peggy and Peggy's Cove, about [how] my great-grandmother was shipwrecked there and how a family by the name of Weaver took her in and raised her. And then she ended up marrying one of the Weaver boys." So Peggy Weaver was it? A fitting name for a young woman whose colourful tale wound its way through generations of family fabric.

It was clear that Maxine's family story echoed the local oral history published by deGarthe. But Maxine had more to tell. After Peggy married the Weaver lad from the cove, the young couple moved to Hamilton, Ontario. Later they moved to North Dakota and began weaving their family fabric below the border. Maxine told me Peggy's descendants are still living there. But how was I to know Maxine was telling me the truth? Why this elderly woman might have read about the shipwreck legend on the back of a cheap postcard and posed as Peggy's direct descendant just to make *me* look bad! It's possible. That's why I played tough and pressed Maxine for proof to support her claims. Oops. She had some.

Peggy's great-granddaughter pulled out a high school essay she had written in Iowa in the late 1930s. I picked it up and read the few lines on the cover:

In Order to Inform Others of My Life for the Past Seventeen Years,
I Write This Autobiography.

Maxine's essay opens with a description that matches the Nova Scotia folk legend published in William deGarthe's booklet. It refers to the shipwreck, Peggy's survival, and subsequent marriage in Nova Scotia.

"I had heard the story [of Peggy]," Maxine said, "so I thought, 'Well, I want to include that.' So I called my aunt in North Dakota and she told me the story."

Maxine had checked her family facts with a reliable source. Her aunt had firsthand access to the Peggy in question, as Peggy eventually settled in North Dakota. Maxine read me the opening paragraph of her testimonial. It amounts to a quick sketch of the original Peggy's family tree:

"On the shores of Nova Scotia, a ship coming from England was wrecked. A family by the name of Weavers [sic] found on the shores that night a small child who was to [sic] young to remember her name. The Weavers reared her because no one knew her identity. After she became of age she married a Weaver [not sic!] and moved to North Dakota. Their daughter married a Miller whose folks came from Holland and settled in Pennsylvania. They had nine children, one of whom was my father. He was named William Henry Miller."

Peggy's daughter, a Weaver, marrying a Miller is perfectly poetic, isn't it? From Weaver to Miller. And now, a Roeper. The ties that bind. Maxine gave me a copy of her interesting family tree. She and her husband hoped to add to it by researching at the Public Archives of Nova Scotia. The genealogical chart shows that Peggy Weaver's daughter was Ella Zedith Weaver, born July 15, 1865 in Hamilton, Ontario. She married Louis Herbert Miller, and had a son called William Henry Miller, born in 1891. Henry was Maxine's father. It's all on the chart.

Now, all of this seems adequate proof from a polite, former pre-school teacher with a gentle smile. Nevertheless, I later called Maxine's older sister in California, to double-check the facts. Mary Ella Miller is listed on the family tree above Maxine. She answered the phone with the same polite, accented voice. Quietly but firmly, she corroborated the entire story I had learned amid the frilly decor of the Teddy Bear B & B.

"Interesting." "Fascinating." But I still had the feeling that something was missing. What happens when folklore becomes fact? Where's the feeling behind the fact? What is really engaging about this story is not simply that Peggy survived and had children who had children. The real drama lies in the inner spark that moved Maxine, so late in her life, to walk the rocks where her family's history began on this continent—the rocks where her great-grandmother escaped a watery death.

"We were out there yesterday and it's quite a place," Maxine told me, struggling to speak. "It's astounding. That sea and the rocks! I can't see how she survived just washing ashore."

"What did you feel as you climbed over those rocks for the first time, at the cove named for your grandmother?" I asked Maxine.

Her eyes filled with tears, her voice wavered. "It was truly exciting. It sent chills up and down my spine, in a way.... I would have loved to have met her."

Peggy's Cove—rocks and surf.

Courageous Captains of Coincidence

An old shipwreck saga of heroism, rescue and unexpected reunions.

I won't blame you if you find this story hard to believe. I might not believe it if I were you. But I do, because I became part of it. So much for objective journalism. This is subjective Know-It-All-ism. When I told this true tale in two parts, on CBC Radio, I was the unwitting coordinator of three emotional meetings between people connected to this human drama. In this story, the medium is the medium. And that's rare. So, get ready for a dramatic sea saga told against the backdrop of bizarre, coincidental connections that could only happen in Nova Scotia. Let us begin.

It was a dark and stormy night. No, really, it was. The three-masted schooner *Hibernia* was sailing through December snow in the Bay of Fundy. Built at Noel, Nova Scotia, the lumber-laden vessel had sailed from Hantsport, heading for Barbados on December 8, 1911. Strong headwinds forced the ship into several ports along the bay. Her last stop was at Beaver Harbour, New Brunswick, where the crew spent Christmas, waiting for a window in the weather. Finally, the window opened. *Hibernia* set her sails for the open seas two days after Christmas, 1911. She never returned.

Soon after entering the open seas, *Hibernia* was badly bruised by a vicious storm off our coast. The ocean poured in on the crew. Clinging to the wrecked hull of their smashed schooner, they were almost swamped by the bone-chilling waters of the Atlantic. An amazing drama ensued. In the terrible storm, the splintered *Hibernia* bobbed like a coffin tossed into the ocean. The sailors survived four cold weeks adrift, thanks to the courageous leadership of their rugged captain. One account tells of the powerful captain maintaining control by forcefully knocking out a panicky sailor. Yet this salty brute of a man had a soft heart. In the midst of desperate despair, *Hibernia*'s captain wrote what he thought would be his last words to his wife; a dying man's final thoughts. He stuffed the letter in a bottle and threw it into the same crashing waves that were smashing his almost submerged vessel. He too was a message in a bottle. A message he had no reason to hope would ever be found. The captain and crew were insignificant debris on the vast dark sea.

I first heard about this unbelievable sea saga from Mr. Kelly Grant in Dartmouth, Nova Scotia. He phoned me in December 1996. It was Mr. Grant's grandfather, a British steamer captain, who happened upon that desperate scene in late January of 1912—a full month after the wreck. Astonishingly the *Hibernia*'s men were still alive! Adrift for weeks in repeated winter storms, the crew suffered no casualties. Grant's maternal grandfather, Captain Philip Tocque, was sailing back to England. Unlike other ships that had come and gone, unable or unwilling to get close enough in rough seas to attempt a rescue, Tocque chose to risk his ship to rescue those desperate sailors. In giving the order to approach the heaving, waterlogged wreckage, Captain Tocque became *Hibernia*'s last hope. Tocque sent a lifeboat out and somehow the half dead sailors got into it. They were brought safely aboard Captain Tocque's steamship. A daring rescue successfully saved all eight of *Hibernia*'s crew!

Clearly both were courageous men and skilled sailors. Their exceptional leadership saved the lives of *Hibernia*'s crew.

The story had piqued the curiosity of Kelly Grant, a retired war veteran living in Dartmouth. He knew that his grandfather, Philip Tocque, was the captain of the rescuing ship but he never knew the name of the captain who had been rescued. Mr. Grant wanted to know whatever became of him after his life was spared so he called me. That's where the story behind this story begins.

First, I phoned the Maritime History Archive at Memorial University in Newfoundland in search of the captain's name. They forwarded a record of *Hibernia*'s sinking. "Vessel abandoned" is scrawled next to the date, January 27, 1912. And there on the page was the captain's name!

Charles E. McDade. Perfect. Now what? Well, my years of on-the-job journalistic training and experience came to my aid. I summoned the finely focussed skills of my proud profession. Nothing happened. So I took a guess. I called up the only McDade I know in this province. It was just a chance but not necessarily a slim one. The interwoven family connections in Nova Scotia often out-distances logical, investigative tactics. It's a uniquely Nova Scotian research method known as "What's your father's name?" That question always leads you somewhere. Sure enough, it worked! My contact, Carol McDade, a local television producer, told me that her father, Bruce McDade, had once mentioned a family ancestor who was involved in a shipwreck. I called him at his home in Sydney and asked him the magic question, "What's your father's name?" I struck out. Or so I thought. Turns out I hadn't gone back far enough. Bruce McDade though told me that his father's father, Charles Edmund McDade, was a sea captain "who nearly drowned in a shipwreck in 1912." Eureka! I made a match. Bruce's grandfather was the captain of the ill-fated schooner *Hibernia*. This

The unlucky *Hibernia*.

was too easy. In one day I had reached both grandsons of the two sea captains who had met under life-threatening circumstances eighty-four years earlier. And these two grandsons, both retired, had lived their entire lives in Nova Scotia without knowledge of the other. That is, until I came along and made the connection through a combination of diligent digging and plain dumb luck. Not necessarily in that order.

Now, step two. I arranged a special surprise telephone link-up, a sort of conference call between the grandsons which would be broadcast on CBC radio. Mr. Kelly Grant of Dartmouth was about to be introduced to Mr. Bruce McDade in Sydney. Actually, in the conversation that followed, both sounded thrilled. It was a special moment. Imagine how these men felt as they reached back into their respective family histories to reclaim a connection forged generations earlier in such dangerous circumstances. In the jargon of the biz, it was "good radio."

"Bruce McDade," I began, "Say hello to Kelly Grant. His grandfather rescued your grandfather." Polite laughter from both men. Then Bruce jumped in. "Mr. Grant, you didn't know that it was Captain McDade." It was a statement and a question, Nova Scotian style.

"I had no idea. That's what struck me [as] strange when I heard this story. There were no local stories about the crew [of *Hibernia*]. But, I figured there must be descendants living."

"Nor did I know that it was Captain Grant that rescued my grandfather!" Now they were getting into it.

"No, Tocque was his name. Captain Philip Tocque."

Bruce addressed me. "This was a surprise to me, too. I share the same sense of mystery about this as Mr. Grant does. To my mind, considering the time at sea, twenty-nine days out in the Atlantic, it's a story that never seemed to get full treatment." I smiled and agreed.

"No, and this is what amazed me," said Kelly, " because you hear a lot of stories about Nova Scotia vessels. It was the twenty-seventh of January that he came across them."

"I want to ask you a question, Mr. Grant," interjected Bruce. "Why was the rescue considered so courageous. Did you know that it was?"

Message in a bottle from the sinking *Hibernia*.

"Yeah. It's in the presentation of this [silver] cup they gave my grandfather. It's in England somewhere. Relatives have it. He had just come through another big gale, you know, the rescue ship, and the seas were pretty bad at the time. It was touch and go whether they could launch a boat or not."

"Right," said Bruce.

"And it was through his seamanship and manoeuvering they were able to launch a lifeboat to get to the schooner," said Kelly.

"When you think about that wreck, that must have been a situation of great preservation and the rescue was one of great sacrifice," said Bruce. It was a nicely balanced summary of events.

"How does it feel to be speaking with the grandson of the man who saved your grandfather?" I asked Bruce.

"It's thrilling really. It's a little extra for me to know that he didn't know and I didn't know and we are making the first contact in eighty-four years."

Kelly answered the same question.

"It's like he says, it's rather thrilling. And the time that has gone by is out of this world. To find out there's somebody still around!"

Bruce chimed in cheerily. "My grandfather waited twenty-nine days for your grandfather. And I waited eighty-four years for you!"

They laughed and talked a while longer. I could tell by their voices that those were meaningful moments for both men. They spoke giddily and gladly about two other men from an older time. Two forefathers who made them proud. Bruce and Kelly swapped details of the wreck and rescue and about each other's salty sea captain grandfather. They were like young boys trading excited stories about their favourite family heroes.

"I understand the ship broke in two!"

"Well, they lost their rudder post and the storm was so severe it swept the three masts off so it was just a floating hulk and they had to work continuously on the three pumps to keep her afloat. For twenty-nine days."

"I have pictures of my grandfather. He was a big man."

"Well, my grandfather was a big man!"

"Well, most of my brothers are six feet or taller."

"Well, you see he had a big family of eight. The four sons were all over six foot. He was a big man himself, very stern. He had a handlebar mustache."

"Well my God! So did my grandfather."

And on they went. Time was up. The two men thanked me and thanked each other. They said goodbye, with a promise to keep in touch. I felt privileged to have listened in on their excited conversation—a classic Nova Scotia moment in the true "What's your father's name?" tradition. They were quite a pair. So were their sea captain ancestors. From the descriptions I had just overheard, I'd say the rescuer and the rescuee were two tough, salty sea dogs, cut from the same sailcloth.

As far as I knew, that was the end of the story. It was enough for me. However, there was more! Part two of the story unfolded a year later. As I reinvestigated the story more strange coincidences of the Nova Scotia variety cropped up. I learned that Bruce McDade's brother, Garnet, had new information about this sea saga. Garnet lived in Hantsport, the same Annapolis Valley port from which his grandfather, Charles McDade, had first sailed, in December 1911. As it turns out, Garnet McDade is an amateur nautical historian. He had information that his brother Bruce didn't know he had. One fascinating article in Garnet's collection is a firsthand account of the sufferings of the desperate crew on board *Hibernia*. The article was written the same year as the wreck, by one of the surviving crew members, Charles Barkhouse. Barkhouse published his account of the ordeal at sea in the Anglican Church parish magazine, in Hantsport. How did it finally come to my attention? That's another coincidence.

I first heard about the Barkhouse article when Kelly Grant called me again. It was a year after he, Bruce, and I had our three-way radio conversation. Mr. Grant told me that he had a copy of the Barkhouse account. Kelly got it from his sister, Gladys Forsyth-Smith, who had been researching her husband's grandfather on a family fact-finding trip in the Annapolis valley in the summer of 1997. Mr. Forsyth-Smith's grandfather was also a Nova Scotia sea captain—we do have lots of seafarers in our past! So the Forsyth-Smiths were researching his sea captain grandfather when they stumbled upon new information about hers. A museum worker directed the Forsyth-Smiths to an amateur nautical historian in Hantsport. You guessed it. He was Garnet McDade, Bruce's brother. Gladys remembered McDade's name from the story told on CBC Radio the previous December. Gladys contacted Garnet and the two enjoyed a conversation as poignant as the one between their brothers. Gladys and Garnet were another pair of grandchildren, of the rescuer, and the rescuee. They met by chance and may never have discovered their connection, had it not been for… well, me! Quite a coincidence. Garnet gave Gladys a copy of the Barkhouse article. Gladys gave the article to her brother, Kelly, who then phoned me. It was a year since we'd spoken and he thought I would like to be brought up to date. The article describes what happened to the sailors who had miraculously survived the *Hibernia* wreck. Clearly there was more to the story that I had told the previous year—a lot more.

I called Garnet McDade in Hantsport to ask him how he came to be in possession of the article written by Captain Barkhouse. (Barkhouse had been ship's mate on the *Hibernia*, although he also had captain's papers.) Garnet told me he had received the article in 1943 through a bizarre twist of fate. He had moved from Parrsboro to Hantsport, Nova Scotia, to begin work in the accounting department at the pulp mill. What followed was another chance encounter. Barkhouse, it turned out, was working just downstairs from Garnet, in the same pulp mill.

"I was only there about two weeks," said Garnet, "when [the superintendent] said, 'Captain Barkhouse, down in the boiler house, wants to speak with you.' So I went down and he asked me if I was Captain Charles McDade's grandson. I told him I was. Tears came to his eyes and he put his arm around my shoulder and told me that they had had a terrible experience at sea together. A few weeks later, Captain Barkhouse met my father—it was a very emotional time for both of them."

Another moving meeting between two people who shared a strange bond because of a terrible event in the past. Call it fate. Call it "meant to be." Or just call it a small province where memories are long. No wait, don't call it anything just yet. There's one more twist of fate to relate.

When I spoke with Kelly Grant about the Barkhouse article, he mentioned his niece, Debbie Forsyth-Smith. She was the daughter of Kelly Grant's sister, Gladys, who got the Barkhouse article from Garnet McDade in Hantsport. Still with me? I recognized Gladys' daughter's name Debbie as an on-air television personality, as they say. I phoned

Gladys Forsyth-Smith in Halifax from Kelly Grant's kitchen. She told me how shocked her daughter Debbie had been, the year before, when she heard me telling this incredible story on CBC Radio. Debbie was certainly interested in the story of her great-grandfather's heroic rescue efforts. But what had bowled her over was to learn that the sea captain her great-grandfather had saved was the great-grandfather of her good friend Carol McDade. Yes, Debbie Forsyth-Smith had worked closely with, and was a longtime friend of, the television producer I mentioned in the beginning. Remember? Carol McDade was my lucky first contact with the McDade family. Carol and Debbie are the great-granddaughters of the two courageous captains, one of whom rescued the other, eighty-five years previously. And they had known each other for years though they didn't know that they shared this captain connection. Carol never knew that she owed her existence to the rescue efforts of her friend Debbie's great-grandfather. This is getting weird isn't it? But I suspect that these coincidental connections could continue *ad infinitum* in Nova Scotia.

I was about to conclude this story right here, but there is one thing I forgot to mention. It concerns the Barkhouse article. The article, published in 1912, is titled *Thrilling Experience of the Shipwreck and Rescue of a Parishioner.* The story describes *Hibernia*'s horrendous saga. When the stern broke open and water poured into the hold, the men ran ropes and tied themselves to the mooring bits so they wouldn't be washed overboard. *Hibernia*'s hulk was barely above the surface. Perhaps more raft than ship, large pieces of the schooner were ripped away like limbs from a tree. The waterlogged hulk of the vessel was kept barely afloat by the buoyancy of the cargo of lumber lashed to the open deck. Inside the one remaining deck cabin, the crew was running out of food. Near the end, they had only turnips to eat that they boiled in salt water.

Several passing ships tried to get close enough to attempt a rescue, but the seas were too high. One ship stood by for six hours trying to run lifelines to reach the floundering *Hibernia*. That steamer finally gave up and left the Nova Scotian sailors to die. Weeks went by. *Hibernia*'s sailors watched the lights of other ships approach from the dark distance, then pass and disappear. It looked hopeless for *Hibernia*.

At three o'clock in the morning, on January 27 their hopes were revived by the lights of the *Denis*, a British steamship. The steamer's course was altered through choppy waves to skillfully manoeuvre near the derelict vessel. Its captain, Philip Tocque, ordered a lifeboat be sent out to the wreck. Second Officer O. J. C. Lee manoeuvered the lifeboat close enough to *Hibernia* that all the men were able to safely jump from the wreck into the boat. They had made it. Saved at last. On board the *Denis*, Captain Tocque saw that the sailors were warmed and fed. Just in time too. Earlier that day the men were contemplating eating the last food on board *Hibernia*—Barkhouse's cat!

Captain Tocque sailed Captain Charles McDade and crew back to Liverpool, England. The rescuer and his crew were given special gifts from the Canadian government. Captain Tocque was awarded the special silver cup that Kelly Grant had mentioned on the radio. It is still kept in the family by his relatives in England. Captain McDade returned safely home from England to his worried wife in Parrsboro, Nova Scotia. About six months after the lucky captain's return home, a letter postmarked from England arrived in his mailbox. Imagine the amazement of the good captain opening the envelope and reading the desperate words of a dying man, written in his own shaky hand. It was his farewell message to his wife. Miraculously, the bottled letter, like himself, had survived the storm. It too was snatched from the sea by some good soul and returned safely home, to Nova Scotia.

Capt. Charles McDade survived *Hibernia*'s wreck.

"inNOVAtion"

*Nova Scotia teaches the world how
to ship a ship from shore to shore.*

I dislike "The Link." That undulating snake of elevated concrete connecting Prince Edward Island to New Brunswick is a bad influence, in my books. "What God has rent asunder, let no man join together," I say. That goes for Halifax/Dartmouth and Cape Breton too. Ban the bridges. Down with the causeway. It's time we fight for the freedom of ferries and for shipdom everywhere! The Confederation Bridge leaves us, high and dry, away from the ocean waves that moulded our maritime heritage. If you must have a link, build a land-link, one that caters respectfully to ships; one that carries ships—portage style! This is not an original idea.

Nova Scotia was a pioneer in such ship-shipping technology. One was almost built on the Isthmus of Chignecto, that place where the rest of Canada becomes Nova Scotia. The plan was to carry ships across land from the Northumberland Strait to the Bay of Fundy—by train!

The sod-turning for this complex ship-railway took place October 9, 1888. To get the lowdown I called John McKay, a retired military engineer in Amherst, who has studied the history of this system of piggy-backing ships. He was happy to speak with me.

"The object was to literally lift the fully-laden ships out of the water in a lifting dock," he explained. "Bring them up to track level, hook onto them with a couple of extra special locomotives, and pull the ship and cargo across the isthmus to a similar facility on the other side, lower it into the water and it could be on its way."

Now *that's* the first class treatment our noble nautical vessels deserve. Not death by Link. If you were sailing from Montreal to Boston, cutting across our isthmus would save you up to seven hundred miles of sailing. This ingenious rail shortcut was designed by Henry Ketchum. (He-was-from-New-Brunswick-but-let's-not-dwell-on-that.)

It sounded like a great idea, but by 1891, the land-link for ships was sunk. "It got 75 per cent finished," said John McKay. "The rails were laid for fourteen of the seventeen-mile length of the line. Then their financing fell through and everything stopped."

And so Henry Ketchum gave up and the project was never completed. (Did I mention he was from New Brunswick?) Rail remnants remain.

"You can still see the outline of the lifting dock and the holding basin in the mud on the Fort Lawrence end of the railway," said John McKay.

But influence flows from failure. Ask any Nova Scotia politician. Planners of the great Panama Canal made construction decisions based on lessons learned from our failed ship-railway. Nova Scotia helped dig the Panama Canal! Even our flops are successful.

Long live shipdom! Down with The Link! (Except on long weekends.)

A Silent Sentry for a Century

Puppy-love enchants a senior sister at a sacred school.

Unconditional love anchored in concrete. What an image! It exists in the still life form of a bright-eyed pup who has warmed the hearts of hundreds of school children for over one hundred years.

He looks alert and awake, lying inside the black iron fence of Halifax's venerable Sacred Heart School—a still and silent sentry.

Sister Margery Lanigan is perhaps this faithful dog's oldest school chum. She patted and "rode" him when she (and he) were much younger. "I was a child here at school myself," she told me. "So I knew of him right straight along since well, what?… 1910?" She has since taught every grade in the Catholic girls school. Now at age 93, she lives next door in the home for Sisters of the Sacred Heart.

Sister Lanigan doesn't go outside much any more. But she ventured carefully across the schoolyard with me to revisit this childhood memory that she's never left.

"He's much loved. He's loved still today and still the children love to come and have a ride on him," she said, looking over the dark sculpted shape with a cheery smile.

"It came from the Convent of the Sacred Heart in Saint John, New Brunswick. And when [they] had to sell it, there were two dogs and a lion and other statues around the property. So one dog was sent to Halifax, the nearest convent, and the other dog and lion went to Montreal."

Sacred Heart School's famous pup.

That happened in 1897.

The dog has certainly endured a lot in his century of service here. From time to time, other dogs are fooled, and challenge him with growls. One time he went missing and his heavy, metal bulk was found atop Citadel Hill. One night, under the cover of darkness, he was painted pink. Jealous university students obviously thought the elementary kids were hogging the dog. After that the savvy Sisters planted the pup in a concrete base where he's been for the last thirty years.

"Oh, he's been everywhere I tell you… in Dalhousie, and in St. Mary's. Oh, he's had a great life," Sister Margery recounted with a knowing glint in her eye, discernible even through thick lenses.

That sparkle in Sister Margery's eyes tells me this pup is alive.

"We love him and he's been a great ad for us all along. We don't do anything to him but pat him. He likes to be patted, you can see that."

Yes, somehow, I *could* see that.

What's in a Dingle?

A twisting trip to the top of a tower.

O ne of my favourite Gaelic words is "dingle," as in "Give me a dingle." Which is just what Sir Sandford Fleming did. He gave Nova Scotia that tall, stone bell tower on the edge of the North West Arm of Halifax Harbour.

Allan Doyle is a well-informed Department of Tourism type who agreed to climb with me up the winding stairway to the tower's top. A climb of ten storeys!

" 'Dingle' is an Irish-Gaelic term which means 'forested cove,' " Allan said, anxiously placing his foot on step one. Our voices echoed up the spiralling, wrought-iron stairs. "You'll notice the various plaques on the walls as we ascend… (Huff, Huff).… They were presented from various institutes, universities, and government agencies within the British Empire.… And of course… (Puff, Puff)… I'm running out of breath here." We stopped. Every small step seemed like a giant leap, and there were more to be climbed.

The Dingle Tower.

Allan decided to buy time by telling me about… time. "Sir Sandford Fleming," he panted, "is world-renowned for setting up the Standard Time zone system at Greenwich, England. He gave us the time of day and we loved him for it." Allan was good-humoured even if short-winded.

In huffs and puffs, he described how Fleming arrived in 1845 to survey for the Canadian Railroad. Time zones were of the essence on that project. The "forested cove" on which the dingle stands was Fleming's cottage country. His columned bungalow remains there today. When he donated the land all he asked in return was that the dingle be erected to mark 150 years of representative government in Nova Scotia.

Queen Victoria's son, the Duke of Connaught, sailed up the Arm on his yacht to give the tower royal assent. Meanwhile, our royal ascent of the tower continued. Allen bravely pushed onward and upward. What a sport.

Finally we reached the belfry. It was a breathtaking view. Unfortunately the climb up the dingle had already taken our breath away. We looked out over the treetops for a time. Then I broke the news. "Allen," I said, "we have to go back down." He smiled weakly.

"Ohhhh. Let's see if we can ride the banister."

A Royal Near-Death Experience

A memorable misadventure of a prince at play in our province.

"Canada's Ocean Playground." You might remember seeing that happy boast on Nova Scotia licence plates. The feel-good catchphrase is meant to tickle the travel fancy of tourists. Sure, it's a slogan, but the spirit of those words was alive long before vacation marketing; even before licence plates. Because, before the turn of the century, Nova Scotia was a play place—for a prince. A playground province by the seashore. Yes sir, we were one big sandbox and water slide for Britain's young Prince George, later King George V, ruler of the British Empire. He was the grandfather of our present monarch, Queen Elizabeth II.

However in the 1880s, George was just a prince in line for the throne, who played and nearly drowned here. Happily, one fast-footed, quick-thinking Nova Scotian saved his life, forever affecting the course of Royal lineage in the British Empire. How do I know this? Ah, therein lies the magic of this playground province. Nova Scotia is a place of ancestral memory; a place of folk tales from old families. A place of oral and aural history. Generations regenerate here. Lives are relived in words and preserved in story, handed down from elder to child. The surrounding ocean erodes our shores, but not our memories. That is why, in the 1990s, I was able to reach back to the desperate, dangerous day in the early 1880s, when Prince George narrowly escaped death in Nova Scotia.

I travelled back in time with help from Susie MacLean. Her father was Neil MacLean, the Nova Scotian who saved the future King of the British Empire. The youngest of seven MacLean children, Susie is now the only surviving offspring of our hero. But she has carefully recorded and shared with her children the story of her father's brush with royalty.

Prince George met Neil MacLean on one of his jaunts into the interior of the province, away from his naval vessel. The young prince was a midshipman on board HMS *Canada*, a British navy vessel sent to patrol our waters. Built in 1881, she was a third-class cruiser, weighing 2,380 tons, with ten six-inch guns and 370 men on board, including the quiet, unassuming prince. The prince was described by a fellow messmate, Everard Fielding, in a 1935 edition of a publication called *The Blue Peter*: "Kindly, honourable and considerate in his dealings with others; rigorous in his duties and highly competent and painstaking in his job as an officer." It would have been a tragic loss had this young royal sailor died on Nova Scotia soil. But he survived. Just barely.

His ship, HMS *Canada* crossed the Atlantic to join the North American Squadron at Halifax. Prince George was promoted to sub-lieutenant on his nineteenth birthday. Old enough to know better, he got himself in trouble anyway.

Neil MacLean was about the same age as the nautical prince. He was helping his parents run the Somerset House, an inn at Hubbards on Nova Scotia's south shore. Racheal and Neil senior also ran the stagecoach line that travelled between Mahone Bay and Halifax. One day when the coach pulled up to the inn, out stepped Francis Durrant, captain of HMS *Canada*. The captain introduced the innkeepers to his midshipman, Prince George of England. Susie MacLean remembered details of that meeting from stories her father had told her when she was a girl. "Dad was very nervous." said Susie. But the prince was very "common" towards her father and tried to put Neil at ease.

When the prince heard that the nearby Dauphinee Mill Lake—now called Mill Lake—was a fine fishing spot, he and his captain decided to spend the night at the inn, hoping to drop a hook the next morning.

Susie didn't say why the captain had taken his princely charge away from his ship on this little jaunt into Nova Scotia's interior. Perhaps it was the prince who was taking the captain? Whatever the reason, there they were, at her grandparents' inn. The next day Neil MacLean rented a rowboat and took the prince and the captain out on the lake. They fished. They laughed. They saw a log boom. MacLean decided to tie up to the logs, climb out of the boat and show (off?) the prince some of his Nova Scotia logging skills. The fancy footwork that followed must have been quite a show. Fit for a king perhaps—or at least a prince. Susie described how her father stepped lightly from one bobbing log to another. Stopping on the largest log at the end, he turned quickly and danced his way safely back to the boat. Well, you just don't put on a slick performance in front of a daring young naval prince whose captain is watching, without triggering the male ego. George decided he could go one better. If a colonial lad could do it, so could he. It's as easy as falling off a log.

Perhaps the proud prince didn't want to be outdone. Besides, log-hopping looks fun. Why not? This is Canada's ocean playground isn't it? "He did jump a few logs," Susie said, "while Dad called out instructions to him." But the promptings of the back-seat logger didn't help. The prince pranced. MacLean and the captain held their breath. Then it happened. While turning around on the big log at the end, the prince slipped on the slick surface. In the blink of an eye, "He went down between the logs." Captain Durrant's heart with panic probably palpitated. The future of the British Empire had just disappeared beneath a bunch of logs in a remote lake in a distant colony! Durrant was his senior officer and therefore was responsible for the safety of the prince. I can almost hear the gulp in his throat. No doubt visions of plank-walking danced in his head. Whatever the dumbfounded Durrant's next move, Neil rose to the occasion.

"Dad was out of the boat instantly," said Susie. "He got to the log where the prince went down and was able to grab a hold of him. Dad struggled and struggled till he got him back into the boat." Whew! Close call. A near-death experience of Royal proportions in rural Nova Scotia. Not too smart. You can lead a prince to water but you can't make him think.

"They rushed home to get the prince in dry clothing and settle him down. It probably took longer for Captain Durrant." No kidding. The prince can almost drown and then just change his pants. Poor Durrant probably lost a year off his life. The future of the Royal Family and of his naval career had almost sunk before his eyes. He probably had to change his pants too! Too close for comfort. Neil saved the prince. God save the Queen.

In 1976, Susie MacLean wrote down her father's story about rescuing the man who would be king. She sent her story to Prince George's granddaughter, Queen Elizabeth II. In response, she received no grand reward for her father's life-saving deed. No handsome payment for saving the Queen's granddaddy; for maintaining the royal lineage; for preserving the Royal Family's proper progression. No, in reply to her letter, Susie MacLean of Hubbards, Nova Scotia received just a brief note from Buckingham Palace written in the hand of the Queen's lady-in-waiting. Ha! She even has someone to do her waiting for her! Anyway, on stationery bearing the crest of Windsor Castle, the note reads as follows:

> *"I am commanded by The Queen to write and thank you for your letter, and to tell you how interested Her Majesty was to hear the story that you enclosed about King George V. The Queen was so touched that you should have sent her this story, and I am to thank you very much for your kind thought."*

Well, it is the thought that counts.

Rockin' by the Lake

Riding the rocking stone of Rockingstone.

After nearly drowning in Nova Scotia's Mill Lake, young Prince George turned to a safer distraction in our province. He abandoned the log-roll for rock and roll. A decade or so after his big splash in the lake, the prince, older and hopefully wiser, tried Nova Scotia's great rocking stone of Rockingstone. The outdoor pastime enjoyed by many Nova Scotians at Rockingstone was a safe attraction, even for a prince. And the rock ride is still there.

The rocking stone is an enormous, weighty bulk of granite perched beside Kidston Lake, in the Spryfield area of Halifax. This monolith is balanced on one of its granite bumps on a flat surface of yet more rock. It's about twelve feet high and wider than it is tall. Always teetering, never toppling, this boulder was deposited in its tricky position by glacial ice, ages ago. Realizing that something so heavy is balanced so delicately is destabilizing. It doesn't seem possible. But there it is and it really does rock. I tested it myself, with a friend. A large log lever jammed under this massive stone rocks the cradle. When I jumped up and down on it, both my friend and I saw it sway. Five or six burly Victorian gentlemen on that lever would likely cause it to rock and roll. In the 1890s, Victorian ladies in big hats would ascend the monster stone by ladder. They would sit down in the sunshine to enjoy the motion while the men below rocked them ever so gently. Ah, those wild Victorians.

Perhaps because the expression "rock and roll" wouldn't be coined until the 1950s, this rock actually didn't. Roll that is. It was perfectly safe. It just rocked on its naturally formed fulcrum. The old *Acadian Recorder* newspaper reported it as among the largest "perched" stones in the world. Someone is tracking perched stones?

Sunday afternoon thrill seekers of long ago would often make the six-mile trek from Halifax to the rocking stone just for the fun of it.

The rocking stone's magic action was first discovered back in 1823 when fishermen made the discovery on a rainy day. Elsie Kidston Morash, who knows much about Rockingstone, told me the story.

"There's a little cavity in the back of the rock. They crawled in there to avoid a storm and the rock began to move; it scared them to death."

Elsie has known that story since her childhood. She also knows about the time Prince George stopped to ride the boulder. This future king apparently had a pleasant and safe see-saw on the stone. Not a death-defying feat like his folly at the lake. Just a tame outing and a quiet walk through the woods, before returning to his ship. At the time the prince was serving in the British navy and during this visit to Nova Scotia he stopped for tea at Elsie's father's farmhouse. For the Kidstons, it was a tremendous thrill! Royalty in the house! It's the kind of event a Nova Scotian family would remember for, well, over a hundred years. Again, preserving the past in the present is the Nova Scotia way. Ancestral memories in this province are cherished like a grandmother's fine china or great granddad's hand-whittled toy boats. Memories and memorabilia are both carefully kept for special times and displayed for younger family members to marvel at. The next generation does the same for their children. And so it goes.

A lady enjoys a rocking ride on the rocking stone. I really like the hat.

Elsie also remembers the time that her father built a road to the rock and charged five cents admission. A little nickel to sit on a lot of granite. I guess that's fair. The rock was on his land, and the rocking stone proved popular enough for John Kidston to make a bit of money to pay for the new road.

Elsie showed me an old souvenir ceramic teapot with a picture etched on it, showing the rock, the ladder, and the lever (or are those the three bones inside the ear? I can never remember). The ladder is gone now. But the stone and the lever remain. So, despite the playground rhyme about what sticks and stones may do to you, try it! If you are someone who likes to rock, take Rockingstone Drive behind Rockingstone Heights Elementary school to the rocking stone, in the area of Halifax known as... yup, Rockingstone.

Tell the rock I sent you. And have a prince of a time!

All Human Life Began in Nova Scotia

The uncelebrated Bluenose scientist who discovered the power of DNA.

"Oswald Avery was perhaps the greatest scientist this century *not* to have received a Nobel Prize," wrote Dr. Alan G. Clamp, lecturer in life sciences at Bexhill College, Bexhill-On-Sea, East Sussex, England, in 1996.

"Who the heck was Oswald Avery and what's he got to do with us?" I wondered when I first heard about this amazing scientist. The answers I uncovered told an intriguing story. A shocking Nova Scotia connection.

It's simple to say but incredible to hear. This Avery fellow was the man who identified the basic substance that is central to all life on the planet. He was the first in the world to learn the scientific secret of heredity, the first to discover the essence of our genetic make-up—DNA! It was revolutionary. One of the most important scientific breakthroughs in history. And this ingenious, hardworking, inventive man-of-science was born and bred in Nova Scotia.

I had no idea that such a crucial cresting in the tide of historical science had formed on a home grown wave. Here, in rustic, rural, historical, hysterical, wonderful, blunderful Nova Scotia. I'll bet you didn't know either. But now you do and pride is permitted. Yes, this great scientist's own DNA was formed in our capital city. Dr. Oswald Theodore Avery was born in Halifax, Nova Scotia, on October 21, 1877. His early intellect was formed by Nova Scotia educators. His determination and dedication were formed within the household of a Nova Scotian immigrant family. Think about it. Dr. Oswald Avery is Nova Scotia's connection to every human being on the planet! Now *there's* a sizeable demographic for a tourism promotion. "Come to Nova Scotia. It's in your genes." Or, "Nova Scotia: Canada's Ocean Gene Pool." Our target market is… everybody!

This is not hyperbolic information. It's the plain truth. And, actually, I was called by a team of scientists to investigate this one. Dr. Martin Willison, a biologist at Dalhousie University in Halifax, wrote me a note posing two profound questions: "Where did Oswald Avery, the discoverer of DNA as genetic material, live in Halifax as a boy and where did he go to school?" I was amazed. Martin had just dropped in my lap the phenomenal fact that a Nova Scotian had discovered DNA's genetic power and he wrapped this revelation in a simple trivia question! Willison knew that the man who was first to identify the genetic stuff of life lived here, in Nova Scotia, and all he wanted to know was which house he had lived in! Which *house*? What about the man himself? What's his story?

Incredulity aside, the house-hunt did sound like fun. So I accepted the challenge, hoping to find Avery's story while I searched for his house. Sometimes I *can* do two things at once.

Dr. Oswald Avery.

But Dr. Willison wanted his school too. That was three things. No problem. I accepted the challenge.

On closer inspection, Martin's note revealed that the request to find Avery's house actually came from Wales. An overseas colleague of Martin's sent a journal article about Dr. Avery to the geneticists of Dalhousie University. Dr. Jim Davies suggested in his letter that Dalhousie scientists do the right thing and put a plaque on Dr. Avery's Halifax home—a meagre replacement for a Nobel prize! And if these great minds wanted to affix a plaque to an old house in Nova Scotia, then, gosh-darn-it, it was my duty to help. The hunt would prove exciting. But first, curiosity demanded that I find out who this Bluenose-born scientist was and how he came to change history.

Dr. Oswald Avery was a quiet, methodical man; scrupulous, diligent, ethical and even musical. He played the cornet—a kind of wide, short bugle—quite expertly when he was young. But he certainly didn't blow his own horn when he made major scientific breakthroughs in his labwork. That's likely why you've never heard of him.

Avery spent thirty-five years in a laboratory at the Rockefeller Institute in New York. That's where he identified deoxyribonucleic acid (DNA) as the central building block of life. Scientists already knew that DNA existed but they didn't know what it did until our man Avery made that momentous link between the two.

Avery may have inherited his scientific mind from his inventive paternal grandfather. Joseph Henry Avery lived and worked in England. He was a papermaker in charge of paper manufacture for Oxford University. He was the first to make thin "bible" paper that could be printed on both sides and was used, of course, for the Oxford Bible. On May 17, 1881, the delegates of Clarendon Press at Oxford presented Dr. Avery's grandfather, Joseph, with a special Bible. It was a gift to acknowledge services rendered during the publication of the revised version of the New Testament. Two sides to every story. Divine invention! So, this knack for inventive investigation was in Avery's genes.

As for being born in Victorian Halifax, that was divine *intervention*.

Dr. Avery's father was a man with a mystical nature. Joseph Francis Avery was born in Norfolk, England in 1846. He came under the influence of a Baptist evangelist, C. H. Spurgeon, who was conducting religious meetings in England. So Avery became a Baptist minister. He married Elizabeth Crowdy, performed three years of pastoral service in England, and then moved with his wife to Nova Scotia because, according to Avery, God told him to. He claimed that God sent him a message which the minister recorded in his journal: "You are wanted and must go to Nova Scotia." Amazing. I've seen T-shirts that read, "Nova Scotia, God's Country," but I didn't take them literally. Frankly, that journal entry rattled me. Could this uniquely located seaport province, this geographical bundle of human wonder, worry and wisdom actually factor so prominently in the Almighty's plans? I'm a person of faith. At least I like to believe I am. Could the Good Lord have chosen this province as the place for Oswald's birth? Was this location crucial to a divine plan for the scientist who introduced the world to DNA's life power? Considering those questions carefully, let's look at the story of Dr. Oswald Avery's birth. It's a little like a story that unfolded… about two thousand years ago. So, stop me if you've heard this.

Dr. Avery's father, *Joseph*, claimed that he received a message that he should take his wife to Nova Scotia. After a long journey the Averys reached the city and, in humble surroundings, they had a male child who would grow up to reveal truths about the nature of life that would drastically advance our understanding of ourselves. Sound a little *dèja vu*-ish to you? Well, it could be that God recycles his plan from time to time. So, the Averys' move to Halifax in May of 1873 might just have been a case of divine intervention. Joseph Avery's journal writings certainly make that claim.

Avery's journal is quoted in his son Oswald's biography, written by Oswald's friend and associate, René Dubos. Avery senior seemed unfazed about sailing across the ocean with his wife, to start a new life.

"Trusting in God's leading. Confident a Church and work awaited on the other side."

Sure enough, one day his steamer tied up at Halifax and the following Sunday, Joseph Avery was asked to preach at the city's North Baptist

Church. He soon became its pastor, and a year later he started his own church which he called the Tabernacle. Avery preached on and off at the Tabernacle until 1887. All indications are that the parents of our DNA identifier were popular and successful in Halifax. Avery's mother, Elizabeth, worked hard to make the church a social centre for the Baptist community. Four years after they settled in Halifax, Elizabeth gave birth to Oswald. Young Ossie—the nickname didn't stick for long—was an independent child. He was small for his age and had his mother's strong intelligent face. From a young age Oswald threw himself into the activities of the church with the same determination that would serve him well later in the lab.

Baptist discipline in Victorian Halifax shaped Oswald's career as surely as did his brilliant mind.

Faith was strong in the Avery family. In 1882, at their Halifax home, Oswald's mother had a near-death experience. Elizabeth Avery was thirty-nine when she took sick with fever and chills. Oswald and her two other sons, Ernest and Roy, stood by her bedside and prayed with their father. Elizabeth eventually fell unconscious. Her body stiffened and grew cold. Her jaw fell slack. The doctor pronounced her dead. Two hours later, Elizabeth miraculously woke up. Soon she was drinking tea and recounting her deathly experience. She said she was told that it was not yet her time. She was disappointed. So Oswald was immersed in the mystical nature of the family's spirituality from his earliest years.

Part two of the divine plan saw Oswald's family moving to New York when he was ten—closer to the scientific resources he would later need to build his scientific knowledge. Oswald's father again wrote that God sent them there. This time Avery's mission was to work with the poor in New York's lower East Side. The Averys again made their "temple" a busy social centre. Avery senior dabbled in medicine, inventing a patented preparation called Avery's Auraline, "for the relief and cure of deafness, earaches and noises in the head." Divine medication? Unfortunately, it didn't sell well.

That New York Baptist community was close despite the degeneracy and chaos of New York city.

When Oswald was fifteen, his father died and his mother went to work with the Baptist City Mission Society, near the Manhattan Bridge. There she came to know wealthy New York women who, like her, were doing charity work. Because of the friendships which ensued, Oswald was able to spend time at some of the greatest estates in New York, including the Rockefellers, the Vanderbilts, and the Sloans. From slums to Sloans. Quite a childhood experience for Oswald.

The New York Male Grammar School primed Avery for Colgate University where he earned his BA in 1900. A Bachelor of Arts! You don't know how good that makes me feel. Yes, BA grads *can* do great things. Maybe there's hope for me yet. Maybe someday I'll get published.

Oswald went on to get his degree in medicine. He practised for three years, then moved to the laboratory.

Oswald soon became known as "The Professor," a nickname that stuck for the rest of his days. Much better than "Ossie," don't you think? Since he grew up knowing the Rockefellers, it seems appropriate that he joined the Hospital of the Rockefeller Institute for Medical Research. In the Institute's laboratory, Avery made his great discovery with help from two junior researchers—Maclyn McCarty and Colin M. MacLeod, a Cape Bretoner from Port Hastings. We Bluenoses do get around, don't we? Not one, but two Nova Scotians played a part in discovering that DNA is our genetic blueprint. A Bluenose blueprint. Hey, the world owes us a living, literally.

It was January 1944, when Oswald and his two aides published their findings in the *Journal of Experimental Medicine*. The authors were cautious when it came to interpreting their results. They did not specifically identify DNA as genetic material. However, in a now-famous letter to his younger brother Roy, a bacteriologist, Avery did speculate along those lines. "Sounds like a virus—may be a gene," he wrote. Subsequent chemical analysis revealed that the agent Avery had isolated was in fact deoxyribonucleic acid—DNA. Avery's findings were correct: DNA was the key to genetic transformation that causes life. But his findings were controversial. At the time, DNA was considered too simple a structure to encode genetic information. Protein was considered the powerhouse! Many refused to accept Avery's discovery. The issue was still contentious when Avery retired in 1948. But a few years later, the celebrated Watson-and-Crick team finally eliminated any doubt when they discovered the actual structure of DNA. The Watson-and-Crick discovery confirmed that Avery's discovery was truly a landmark in genetics. Their work on the building blocks of life was itself built on a scientific foundation of blocks laid by Oswald Avery of Nova Scotia. Yet when Avery died at age seventy-seven, February 20, 1955, the scientific world was still celebrating Watson and Crick's work. Sadly, there was not much mention of our Nova Scotian scientist.

Today Avery's genius is more widely recognized. "He's very well-known," I was told by Dr. Bob Lee, a genetic biologist in Halifax. "He's taught in our first-year genetics class. Any book on genetics discusses Avery's work. He had a major impact on the development of the field, and he opened the door to modern molecular genetics. The only thing he didn't get was a Nobel Prize." But Watson and Crick got one for their work, which piggy-backed Avery's findings. Why were those two Nobelized and not Avery? Dr. Lee told me it came down to poor public relations on Avery's part. Oswald was brilliant but shy. He was a complex, introverted person. When he published his paper he didn't market it as Watson and Crick did. You see, Watson and Crick published their great discovery in a popular journal, *Nature*. They titled it simply and clearly: *A Structure for DNA*. Our friend Avery, on the other hand, had published his paper in a more conservative medical journal and gave it the awkward title, *Studies on the Chemical Nature of the Substance Inducing Transformation of Pneumococcal Types*. The less-than-sexy subtitle was, *Induction of Transformation by a Deoxyribonucleic Acid Fraction Isolated from Pneumococcus Type Three*. My guess is that nobody read the paper, in fact I'd wager no one got past the title. Poor Dr. Avery. No one told him to sell the sizzle with the steak. So, no Nobel. Maybe placing a plaque on his Nova Scotia birth-home would make amends. Wait, isn't that where we started out? I forgot the question that got me started on this. The original request was to find out where in Halifax Oswald Avery had lived and where he went to school.

Historian, expert genealogist and leather-jacketed biker, Terry Punch, came to the rescue. Terry checked his collection of city directories for the 1870 period. Garry Shutlak, at Nova Scotia Archives and Records Management produced city fire insurance records from the 1880s. Three Avery household addresses were listed.

Armed with an archival arsenal of addresses I started the house-hunt. First stop, Dr. Avery's birth-home of 1877. Number 18 Moran Street in Halifax. It's an old short street, just north of historic Citadel Hill, between Agricola and Robie Streets—a stone's throw from the Halifax Armoury building. But don't risk throwing stones at the Armoury—it has soldiers in it.

I invited the Dalhousie genetics professor, Bob Lee, and his research assistant to come along for the hunt. Three of us in search of the wise man's home. The excitement inside my red Dodge Colt skyrocketed as we neared the location. Genetic biologists can get quite eager.

"There's Sarah Street." "Keep going." "Oh, there it is." "Is that 'One Way'?" "Okay, there it is." This was high-tech scientific research. "According to the 1877 City Directory, he lived at 18 Moran Street. And there's number 2381!" We were off by a couple thousand houses. No, actually we were off by a century or so. House numbers are like house prices—considerably higher today. But my archival experts concluded from their diagrams and documents that the fourth building from the north-west street corner was the Avery house. Today it is number 2370, a flat-roofed house with white vinyl siding and a Beware of Dog sign in the window. Dr. Lee looked like he was about to say something very scientific. "Amazing… wow," he said. "That's the house to plaque." Then we went on to find the other houses the Averys had lived in. The next stop was a nondescript house at 248 Gottingen Street near the liquor store. In 1887 they moved to a site on Robie Street where there is now a Mazda dealership.

I relied on Terry Punch's encyclopedic knowledge of historical Halifax to determine where Oswald Avery went to school. Judging from the Robie Street site, where Avery lived during his early school years, he likely attended Almon Street Elementary located just two blocks from where his house once was.

Five months after I told this story on CBC Radio, I received an unexpected call from another science professor at Dalhousie University. He wanted to verify the correct house number. He also invited me to a fund-raising dinner to raise money to purchase the plaque for Dr. Oswald Theodore Avery's historic Halifax birth-home. Good for them. The plaque may not be a Nobel, but it will be noble; Nova Scotian scientists remembering one of their own. And besides being noble, the plaque should be wide. After all, someone is going to have to etch "deoxyribonucleic acid" on it!

The Klonðike Kíngs

*One launched the great gold rush
and the other reaped the spoils.*

One hundred years ago a prospector yelled, "Gold!" The famous Klondike gold rush had struck; the panning, the panic, the people. What a rush! Thousands hiked into the Yukon to dig and discover. The population exploded as folks flocked to find their fortunes, each in search of those magic nuggets that would change their lives forever. It was the great get-rich-quick craze of the century. And it was a brilliant geologist from Nova Scotia who predicted and pinpointed the great deposits that made men millionaires.

This Nova Scotia connection fascinated me. Late in 1997, I received a little Internet nugget that inspired me to dig further into this claim. All the way from the Yukon itself, this note was quite something:

"Hi. On this, the eve of the 1998 centenary celebration of the Klondike Gold Rush, I thought this question might interest your listeners and pique your interest. What is the connection between Dawson City, Yukon and Pictou, Nova Scotia?"

It was signed, "A transplanted Maritimer, Scott Wilson, Whitehorse, Yukon, Canada."

Scott had "gone down the road" about as far as a Maritimer can go, and still he encountered a Nova Scotia influence. Yes indeed, a Pictou County boy was responsible for the great Canadian Gold Rush of 1898. He was the brilliant geologist who predicted the enormous deposits of Klondike gold. His brilliant reports and geological maps were used by soon-to-be rich prospectors. After gold fever struck the Yukon Territory, a new town was named after this Nova Scotian who helped make it all possible. Dawson City, the township at the centre of the Klondike stampede, was named in honour of George Mercer Dawson, born in Pictou on August 1, 1849. That's right, the man who pointed the way to veins of Klondike gold had veins of Bluenose blood. Not only was he born in Pictou, but he spent his most impressionable years on Nova Scotia soil.

Hopeful prospectors panning for gold.

Aside from revealing the Klondike gold deposits to the world, George Dawson also mapped out Canada's 49th parallel and Alaskan boundaries. His reports on the natural history and resources of Canada's west attracted settlement on the prairies and promoted the expansion of the railway. His glowing reports expounded on the vast coal riches of Alberta. (And we all know how those resources paid off.) George was also first to survey the Rocky Mountains, and was among the first to recognize, study and defend the culture of the Haida Natives. In short, this man from the east was a central influence in developing Canada's west.

George Dawson was a geologist, author, teacher, civil servant, geographer, anthropologist, palaeontologist, poet, and artist. You could say he was some kind of Nova Scotia know-it-all! On top of his incredible scientific skills, George seems to have been blessed with an attractive personality and strong leadership skills. Suffice it to say, George had a lot going for him.

Dawson's middle name came from his mother, Margaret Ann Young Mercer. She possessed the Scots' love of a rigorous education and all her children were well-schooled. George's father, John William Dawson, was an eminent geologist in his own right. He succeeded in his work to bring Nova Scotia's rich geological deposits to world attention. When Dawson senior became president of McGill College in 1855, he took his family from Pictou to Montreal. Six-year-old George Dawson would one day return to the place where he had first explored the natural world as a small boy. Growing up on the wilds of the McGill College grounds, young George learned his science from the ground up, literally. He collected specimens on Mount Royal and worked with his father in the college museum. George's mind was insatiable, curious, and perceptive. His body was another thing. Tragically, George was disfigured early in life by Pott's Disease, otherwise known as tuberculosis of the spine. All of his busy, adventurous life, George Dawson was handicapped by a painful curved spine, resulting in a small stature. Nevertheless, he excelled intellectually and published his first paper when he was just twenty-one. Ambitious, gifted, and well prepared by his father's tutelage and his mother's encouragement, George enrolled in the best scientific education programmes then available. Beginning his studies in Edinburgh, then moving on to the Royal School of Mining in London, George absorbed the intensive training like a sponge. He excelled at a wide gamut of courses: applied mechanics, chemistry, metallurgy, and paleontology, among others. In 1872, George graduated with distinction and was presented with a bucket of medals, prizes, and scholarships. Is this beginning to sound like a personals ad for Superman? Well, it's all true—and there's more.

George had the credentials to begin work anywhere he wanted to, but he decided to return to his roots in Nova Scotia. He was hired by some Bluenose businessmen to test samples of coal and iron ores for their content. He was starting out in his father's field of expertise; Nova Scotia's underground resources. It's likely Dawson senior had some influence in securing the position for George as he had used his contacts to ensure George's enrollment at the prestigious Mining School in London. (That's early evidence of another refined Nova Scotia tradition: influence-flexing.) George was certainly well-qualified for his first geology job. After all, he'd had rocks in his head since birth. Again following his father's footsteps, George eventually took a position teaching chemistry at Morrin College in Quebec. He was later appointed geologist and botanist to the British North America Boundary Commission and, two years later, he became chief geologist for the respected and historic Geological Survey of Canada.

George soon became a leader among second-generation Canadian geologists. For two years he travelled with the survey team across previously uncharted territory of a newly-born Canada, surveying the 49th parallel. His region of study was a swath of land, 800 miles long and 60 miles wide, across the middle of North America. Wow. Thank heavens he didn't have to mow it. He just had to survey it. Still, not an easy task. That's a lot of stones not to leave unturned. But George's multidimensional analysis of the region was hailed as one of the classics

of Canadian geology. He reported on mineral resources, fossils, the natural history of the land, and even collected three hundred specimens of mammals and birds for the British Museum's collections. If geologists have heroes—and I think they should—George Dawson was about to become one.

That early Dawson report argued that the west had very good settlement potential. The area had good agricultural land and lots of it. It also had rich underground resources. George's report was encouraging. (There's a rumour he also wrote "Hey, if you lived here, you'd be home by now!" But that's not been confirmed.) George's work lead other experts to proclaim that a much greater agricultural potential existed on the prairies than even he had expected. But George's work was a key stimulus to Canadian settlement. And all this time we thought it was the beaver!

George's research helped open the west in a second way. For a long time it remained the principal source of geological information used by railway builders. Essentially, George's reports told them where they should lay their track. The train on the plains stayed mainly where he deigned! He not only reported on the best lands for settlement, he helped to map out the best routes for getting there. George Dawson was a country builder. But despite his impressive accomplishments, George was a small man. The ravages of his childhood condition left him with the stature of a twelve-year-old boy; his back remained curved and twisted all of his life. Overcoming his physical limitations, George covered enormous distances of Canada's rocky, rugged western landscape. As the pioneer surveyor of the vast Rocky Mountains, this diminutive, determined geologist was known to have had local natives carry him over rough sections of the trek. Dawson also collected evidence from several western river regions: the Red River, the Assiniboine, and the Souris, as well as the Skeena and the Peace River valleys. This work contributed to debates about ancient glacial movements and how they carved Canada's earth, leaving a legacy of landforms. In geology and geography, George left a deeply carved legacy for Canada.

George also looked outside of Canada in his work comparing evidence of Canadian rock transformations with volcanic activity in Chile! He was practising an advanced form of "theoretical geology." But please, don't try theoretical geology at home. We wouldn't want anyone to get hurt!

George was as skilled at the theoretical side of his science as he was adept at the practical rockhunt. His ability to predict and extrapolate from known facts lead to one of the greatest-ever contributions to Canadian commerce. I learned about this from Dr. Suzanne Zeller, a history of science professor at Wilfrid Laurier University in Waterloo, Ontario. She co-wrote a history of Dawson's life in the *Dictionary of Canadian Biography.*

George, it appears, had a Midas touch. His 1887 Yukon expedition lead to two great Canadian accomplishments. This Nova Scotian marked a location for the much disputed Alaska boundary. He also reported on gold-bearing gravels he discovered. This geological genius extrapolated from that find to predict major gold deposits, miles away in the Klondike River, that weren't discovered until years later. George's keen knowledge of glacial patterns helped him predict possible work-able gold deposits in the Klondike. His written report contained useful geological maps and access routes. Two editions of that report sold out. It was a harbinger of the great Klondike gold rush of the late 1890s. And George had never even set foot on the Klondike site where the gold eventually was found. He was a human divining rod, pointing with a gold finger to the spot where others would dig.

His biographer, Dr. Suzanne Zeller, put it this way:

"His reports were highly regarded for their accuracy, for his brilliance in systematic mapping. He had an uncanny ability to interpret the landscape, especially the geological landscape. And he understood the processes by which gold was formed geologically and was able to suggest the area in which gold would eventually be found. He knew where to look for it. And people read his reports with that intention."

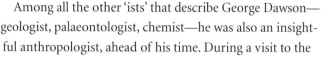

Among all the other 'ists' that describe George Dawson—geologist, palaeontologist, chemist—he was also an insightful anthropologist, ahead of his time. During a visit to the Queen Charlotte Islands he was captivated by the beauty of the Haida totem poles. In their village construction, he saw intelligence and skill. To a lesser skilled geologist, this may have meant little. But George was a Darwinian scientist who perceived a highly evolved culture. Despite his father's staunch anti-Darwinian stance, George had picked up the evolutionary bent in London, under "Darwin's Bulldog," Thomas Henry Huxley.

"George Dawson became T. H. Huxley's star student at the Royal School of Mines," said Zeller. "He won all the prizes in those subjects and came back not having been able to avoid a Darwinian research training in natural history. And he brought this very modern training to his work in geology, in ethnology and so on."

Huxley trained George to see how geographical regions change according to the way species distribute themselves in the land. George shaped that learning into a modern evolutionary approach to his fieldwork. Survival of the fittest was shaped by ridges and rises of rock and river. But George noticed that Haida villages were being deserted as the numbers of natives were diminishing rapidly. That's why George the ethnologist-geologist began adding richly descriptive appendices to his geology reports that would be seen by government. He included a Haida vocabulary in his report on the Queen Charlotte Islands in 1878-79. He encouraged Haida crafts and trades, hoping they could survive in harmony with industries to come with new Canadian settlement. He warned his government that Haida culture had clear concepts of property ownership, which railway developers would have to consider carefully. At least that was his plea, naïve or not. His passion for Haida culture expanded. He photographed and sketched their totem poles, *à la* Emily Carr. He collected artefacts for McGill College. Later, George reported on other BC native tribes, comparing their vocabularies and producing a linguistic map. His ethnological work brought international recognition for his country. He was hailed as a "Father of Canadian Anthropology."

George's early collecting laid some important foundations in Canadian science. The present-day Canadian Museum of Civilization can thank our George for his work which now forms the core of its ethnological department. The present National Museum of Natural Sciences can thank him for his remarkable dinosaur fossil collection, at the centre of the department of vertebrae paleontology. And I would like to thank him for making me have to spell so many big scientific words.

His mastery of many interrelated fields made George a much sought-after expert. Over time, he acquired many prestigious titles: fellow of the Royal Society of London, president of the Ottawa Field Naturalists' Club, director of the Geological Survey of Canada, gold medal-recipient from the Royal Geological Society (and later, vice-president of same), also vice-president of the Canadian Mining Institute, president of the Geological Society of America and associate editor of the *Journal of Geology* in Chicago. George also bagged a collection of honorary doctorates over the course of his career, from Princeton, Queen's, McGill, and Toronto.

He sure came a long way from Pictou County, didn't he? But George Dawson's success was set against one sad, personal failure. George lived his whole life alone. He never married. He fell in love once and proposed marriage, but the young woman's parents refused to let her marry George, citing his physical deformity as the reason. They rejected George's brilliant mind, his academic achievement, his bright future, his handsome face and sensitive personality. Whether or not all that he accomplished filled the void left by his romantic heartbreak, we will never know. The balance of his life was certainly tipped towards an exceptional amount of work and travel. And in the end, his death was exceptional as well. Fewer than eighteen months after his father died,

George succumbed to bronchitis. It was 1901. George was only fifty-two years old. His death was a shock for many who respected his awesome physical and intellectual accomplishments across the country. His greatest legacy was merging theoretical science with practical results. By bridging that gap, George Dawson's science brought a new Canada enormous economic activity and fabulous wealth. But all that glitters is not yet told.

～

There was another Nova Scotian who dominated the Klondike's bonanza period. Just one county over from George Dawson's original Pictou home, lived Alex "Black John" McDonald who would later become one of the first filthy-rich Yukon venturers. In fact, he was given the title "King of the Klondike." He was a Nova Scotian from Ashdale, Antigonish County, and became known as the Big Moose from Antigonish—or Big Alex for short. ("Alex" is pronounced "Alec." It's a rural Nova Scotianism.) His name came both from his success in the gold rush as well as his large physical presence. Big Alex was a mammoth Highland Scot, an awkward, jowly, bulging giant with fists like hams. Historical writer Pierre Berton describes this "elephantine Nova Scotian" in his 1972 book *Klondike; The Last Great Gold Rush 1896-1899*.

"He spoke slowly and painfully, rubbing his blue jowls in perplexity, his great brow almost hidden by a shock of sable hair, his heavy lips concealed by a moustache of vaudevillian proportions. The effect was primeval, but in spite of his Neanderthal appearance, Big Alex was one of the shrewdest men in the North. When others sold, he bought—and he continued to buy as long as there was breath in his body. Within a year he was famous, hailed on three continents as the "King of the Klondike."

Big Alex soared from clumsy labourer to Dawson City aristocrat in no time. He wasn't as interested in the gold itself as he was in property acquisition. He was obsessed. He loved land. Big Alex bought up chunks of land all over the Yukon. His gold claims and business deals were so numerous that when first introduced to a stranger Alex would ask the man if they were business partners. This gruff Nova Scotian entrepreneur introduced the "lay" system into the Klondike. Rather than work a single gold claim by himself, Big Alex owned many and let others do the work. He would let a section of his land out on lease or "lay," then accept a percentage of the miner's find. At times the percentage was half. With this inventive, labour-saving scheme and his deceptively simple oval face, Big Alex made many lucrative deals.

Alex's passion for property and his sharp mind contrasted with his Goliath appearance and his painfully slow, stumbling speaking style. But soon Big Alex owned several buildings in the new boom town named after his fellow Bluenose traveller, George Dawson. He built one building and lived in the top floor. He owned and leased to the government the local Post Office building. This Nova Scotian giant was also big at heart. When the church burned down, Big Alex—a devout Scots Catholic—volunteered the funds to rebuild it. He continued to acquire land from bankrupt prospectors as well as from other bank deals. Much of the land he acquired had workable claims that paid off extremely well. This Nova Scotian's skill in assessing land values came from his time as a buyer for the Alaska Commercial Company. Fourteen years in Colorado's silver mines and a stint on the famous Alaska Panhandle also primed him for his Yukon gold dealings.

There seemed no end to Alex's wealth. And yet, in a place where greed and prices were equally inflated, Big Alex had a surprising lack of concern for the amount of gold he possessed. His property passion was almost a religion. He viewed gold as simply the means to acquire land and more gold claims. In fact, Alex once referred to the glittery riches as "trash." When a woman visited his home in Dawson, Big Alex pointed to a bowl of nuggets he kept on the mantel. He urged the lady to take a handful as if offering chocolates. Yes, Big Alex was different.

Alex travelled to Paris and then to Rome where he was granted an audience with the Pope. A more unlikely couple would be hard to imagine. Nevertheless, Big Alex was made a Knight of St. Gregory for his donation to the hospital in Dawson. Then this huge man, bursting the seams of his formal attire, visited the city of London, where he spent a lot of time riding up and down the elevators (which he called "heists").

Somewhere between the ups and downs, he met twenty-year-old Margaret Chisholm, the daughter of the superintendent of the Thames Water Police. She and her father later emigrated to Canada and she and Alex were married. Her father settled in British Columbia.

Nova Scotia's Big Alex, the King of the Klondike, continued his wealthy but socially awkward position as Dawson's man of property. When Sam Steele, Dawson's celebrated police officer left for a new life in 1899, the townspeople chose Big Alex to make a special presentation at the steamboat. The giant was carefully coached on the words to say as he presented Steele with a poke of gold nuggets. Sheepish and shy, the brute shuffled forward and clumsily thrust the poke into Steele's hand. According to Pierre Burton, Big Alex's carefully prepared speech came out as follows:

"Here, Sam—here y'are. Poke for you. Good-bye."

Ahhh, that's our noble King of the Klondike. Clearly a man of action, not of words. And yet, sadly, his land-buying addiction eventually led to his downfall. Once his major claims were worked out, he bought distant properties that were about as rich in gold deposits as his speech was eloquent. He ended up living in a little cabin by a creek, and although many millionaires would still be made, Alex's own fortunes had diminished. It had been a wild rags-to-riches-to-rags ride for Big Alex. He died penniless in the Yukon—the place that made him rich and famous and the place that he helped make with his riches and fame.

Well, that's historian Pierre Berton's account of Alex's downfall, anyway. But I've heard a different version of his final days in his home county of Antigonish, Nova Scotia. Retired judge, Hugh MacPherson is a wise keeper of local history and folklore in that corner of the province. He told me that his father knew Big Alex, and he himself knew Big Alex's nephew, Charlie, who went to the Yukon to bury his Uncle Alex. The judge told me that the local story was that his great wealth was not entirely lost—it was stolen. Apparently Big Alex's wife, Margaret, conspired with his personal secretary—a male secretary—to empty Alex's safety boxes. They allegedly cleaned him out! So the giant millionaire prospector died broke and alone in an isolated cabin. That's what "they" say. And I often find that the "they" of oral history have a wisdom and accuracy that ought to be respected. Whichever version of history is correct, Big Alex spent his remaining days in the northern land he loved, a land he helped to settle. And either way, he died without the burden of the gold "trash" that he didn't seem to have much care for. Today, Dawson residents remember Big Alex's contribution to their historic town. Tour guides in period costume show visitors through old buildings built by Big Alex's wealth.

It's a twisted saga, that of George M. Dawson and his next-county-over neighbour, Big Alex McDonald. It is the history of Yukon gold itself, of Dawson (the town), and of an exciting Canadian era. It's a saga of science and business, of fame and fortune, reaped and lost, amid the rise and fall of the great gold hunt a century ago; a tale of finders, reapers, losers, keepers. A tale of two Klondike Kings from Nova Scotia.

(Please note that at no time in the writing of this story did I use the expression, "There's gold in them thar hills!" I'm proud of that. Thank you.)

Kilts, Cabers, and Celtic Curses

A Scottish sports commentary.

The Highland hammer-throw event is an ancient Celtic sport, deeply rooted in rich Highland tradition. I decided to try it one day. I was driving big nails into my deck at the time. One slip. One thumb. *Thwack!* Instantly I felt connected with my mystical Highland heritage. The hammer and a few choice Gaelic words flew with all the might I could summon from my Celtic blood. I wept.

That's probably how the ancient Scots developed the hammer-throw event. Their centuries-old Highland games were based on their work.

The modern-day work equivalent might be the computer-throw. (An event I've also tried, and enjoyed.)

Dr. John Hamilton, a past president of the Antigonish Highland Games, explained the Games' origins to me. He helped me understand how and why grown men in plaid skirts try to throw telephone poles. "The competitor picks up a pole about twenty feet long that weighs between 175 and 225 pounds. He balances it on the shoulder, runs a distance and tries to throw it so that it flips end-over-end."

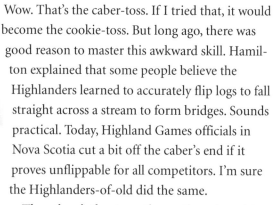

Wow. That's the caber-toss. If I tried that, it would become the cookie-toss. But long ago, there was good reason to master this awkward skill. Hamilton explained that some people believe the Highlanders learned to accurately flip logs to fall straight across a stream to form bridges. Sounds practical. Today, Highland Games officials in Nova Scotia cut a bit off the caber's end if it proves unflippable for all competitors. I'm sure the Highlanders-of-old did the same.

Then there's the stone-throw: throwing a big rock. Again, a practical event if you have a rocky field to clear. Apparently this was a common strength-test among mythological Scottish heroes. Gaelic cursing is optional in this event. The fifty-six-pound weight-throw event uses a solid block of iron with a chain attached, which burly Scots fling for height and distance. Much like my hammer-throw experience on the back deck. My height and distance were very good. Very, very good.

Walk softly, carry a big stick and wear a kilt—a Highland games tradition.

The Antigonish Highland Games predate Canadian Confederation. Nova Scotia's Scots have been tossing and flipping heavy objects there since 1863. It's more than quaint tradition. It's the Scottish Olympics. And it's very competitive.

"You'll find that the throwers of the hammer have great daggers stuck on the front of their boots," said Hamilton, "which they dig into the ground so they can throw the hammer a little further."

Phew. Serious stuff. Maybe I should wear the right gear for the right event too... like a metal glove on my nail-holding hand, while I swing my hammer with the other.

Nova Scotia Nicknames: Naughty and Nice

A guide to the Highland name game of northeastern Nova Scotia.

"What's your faaather's name?" It's a comically clichéd question in Cape Breton, and among Scottish descendants in Antigonish, Pictou, and Guysborough Counties. The soft Scotch drawl on "father" is optional, but common. Should you live among the Gaels and Scots of northeastern Nova Scotia a name is a complex thing. After all, your name is who you are. But it's not that simple. Not in the Celtic corner of our province. There the custom among folks who want to know you is to ask not just your name, but where you got it—your father's name. In the ancient clannish culture it's an accepted way of kindly inquiring, "Who are your people?" "Who do you belong to?" If you think about it, it really shows more interest in knowing *you*, and not just reciting the label you are known by. It's a caring tradition. It's also very handy as a means of identity.

You see, often using one name is not enough if you live among Nova Scotia's multitudinous Mc's and Mac's of Scottish origin; the hundreds of MacDonalds and MacLeans and MacKinnons and McNeils and MacIntyres and MacKenzies and MacIsaacs and McDougals and McKays and MacKays and McEacherns and MacEacherns and

McGregors and MacAskills and McInnis' and MacReadys and MacLaughlins and MacLeods and MacMany, many, more! Keeping up with the Joneses is easy in comparison. There are soooo many people with the saaaame surname. You could go mad amidst the myriad of Mc's and Mac's—not to mention the copious Chisholms and the Gillises and the Frasers and the Etceteras.

That's why a unique nicknaming habit evolved among Scotland's people. A way to identify folks. A way to confidently mix and match the Mc's and Mac's. The results are often entertaining, sometimes cruel, but always useful in telling one old MacDonald from another. Simply referring to the one who "had a farm" might not help. They all had farms!

I set out on a nickname trek to collect some of "Nova Scotia's Wacky Nicknames." (As coined by a 1980 *Reader's Digest* article.) My trek began in small town Antigonish, home of the annual International Highland Games. This is the town of Angus the Nun who worked in a convent and Angus the Priest who worked in a church; where Maggie-in-the-Sky lived on the top floor of the tallest building on Main Street (three storeys!) This is the town where, if your dead husband's name was Alec you might be called Alec the Widow. Better than being mixed in with the Mc- and Mac- masses. Adding an entire family tree to your given name is another approach. A name handed down over generations.

I sat down to a cup of tea with a woman who knows the nickname game firsthand. Mrs. Kathryn D. A. Chisholm invited her friend Bo Chisholm (no noticeable relation) to help explain how the nickname game works. She used her own name as a teaching example.

"My husband… his grandmother was the widow Collin, so his father was known as John Collin-Widow Collin. So that whole family of Chisholms, my husband's people, were known as The Widow Collins."

"But I had always heard that your husband was called by the nickname "Collie Pioneer." I said.

"Oh yeah, well later in life, when he got into construction, their business was Pioneer Construction. So he was known as The Pioneer. And so his partner Donald, Donald Collie Red Archie, was known as The Pioneer too. He had both names." Of course he did. Donald Collie Red Archie The Pioneer! According to the nickname system, having two nicknames made him easier to identify. Yes, I think he would stand out with a handle like that. Had I really got it?

"So, if your husband was Collie Pioneer, you were Mrs. Pioneer?" I asked hopefully. Nope. I didn't quite get it yet. It turns out Kathryn D. A., as she is known around town, is also known as Kathryn Danny Kirk. Why the two names? Two reasons of course. Her father was called Danny Kirk MacDonald because his father, D. A. MacDonald, used to work in New Glasgow with a shipbuilder named Kirkpatrick. So D. A. became known as Danny (D. A.) Kirk-MacDonald. Two generations later, his grand-daughter, Kathryn is known as Kathryn D. A. or Kathryn Danny Kirk, a third-generation Kirk, even though the family's last name has always been MacDonald and they're not even related to the Kirks. Got it? That's one naming method. It took me several cups of tea before I caught on. Perhaps something stronger would have helped. Of course being called "Kirk" meant the family was then confused with a real Kirk family, on the same street. So there was a flaw in the system. Kathryn Danny Kirk remembered that when she was young, down-and-outers would come to her father's front door asking for a bottle to wet their whistles. But they were at the wrong Kirk house. Motivated by mischief or by sympathy, the Danny Kirks always kindly redirected the booze seekers up the street to Ralph Kirk, the local Member of Parliament. An MP, of course, had a harder time "just saying no."

Some of the nickname nomenclature in northeastern Nova Scotia follows a different system. It's less genealogical. Some folks are labelled according to a physical attribute. It's not always nice, but often useful. Bo Chisholm told me about two former policemen in town. Brothers. One with excellent posture, one slightly stooped. One of them was called Six O'Clock.

"He walked so straight, he was straight up and down. Six to twelve! Yeah. He had a brother, Five After Six. He always had a slant on."

Our tea took an hour. There are hundreds of nicknames, especially for men with the all too common name Angus MacDonald. Hence Angus the Smelt, Angus the Senator, Angus the Bank, Angus Tulloch, Angus the Bolt, Angus the Jailer, Angus the Beard, and Angus the Ridge of the Ridge MacDonalds. (No, they didn't work for Pioneer. These pioneer settlers built their original homestead on a ridge of land on Cape Breton Island. The nickname stuck through the generations, even when descendants moved away.) Entire families would be painted with the same brush, such as the Painters; the Gooses; the P. D.'s and the D. D.'s. One of the D. D. MacDonald's was called "Fiddle"; Fiddle D. D. A distinguished officer of the court was quite casually called The Hanging Judge, long after the day of the midtown gallows. A longtime pharmacist at McKenna's Drugstore on Main Street was known to all as Gish. No one really knew why.

Here are more to remember: Jack the Cop. Jenny the Basket. She simply carried a basket—once too often I would guess. Ronnie Elbows MacDonald. He was known for the creative use of his elbows in hockey. Hence, Ronnie Elbows! It's a peculiar name, but when he was elected mayor of the town it stuck out. His Worship, Mayor Elbows? Truth may be stranger than fiction in the Scottish nickname world, but sometimes it's obvious. Long Leo Chisholm was very tall. And Leo Boots Chisholm ran a shoe store. As for Joe Do-Dad, I don't know why he was called that. I'm not sure I want to know.

I had my fill of tea. Saying my goodbyes to the two Chisholms, Kathryn and Bo, I journeyed to the next county to chat with an academic expert in Scotch nicknames.

Off the main highway in Pictou County, I turned on to the old road to Egerton. The name on the rural mailbox read MacKenzie. A long rutted lane stretched up a snow-covered hill to an old white farmhouse. Bare branches of ancient towering trees hung over its roof. A. A. MacKenzie answered my knock. Angus Anthony. He goes by "Tony." Tony is a big Gael with thick hands and a grey bristly brush cut. A "brogueish" Cape Breton lilt to his voice betrayed his Scotsman's blood, as did his strapping size. Inside was pure old world nostalgia. Angus Anthony MacKenzie is a retired academic who lives in his mother's pre-turn-of-the-century farmhouse. The floors are made of wide wooden planks. Thick, rough-hewn beams are angled overhead. A musty smell touched my nostrils as we walked through the cluttered kitchen. The woodstove crackled in the sitting room. The scent of age wafted with the smoke. Tony's books lined the wall by the woodstove.

Tony MacKenzie is a Scottish nickname expert, or at least he's the closest thing to it in academic circles. He was born in Dominion, the son of a Cape Breton coal miner. He taught history at St. Francis Xavier University in Antigonish, before retiring and moving to Egerton, Pictou County. His collection of unique nicknames, naughty and nice, is rich with a variety of styles and methodology. He started by explaining the patronymic style, the inherited nickname, passed down from father to son.

"There was a man up the road here, called Old Young John's Big Johnny's John. That was the first fantastic nickname I ever encountered. His father was Big Johnny. His grandfather was Young John. His great grandfather was Old John. You can figure it out."

And so I could. I was surprised. I was beginning to understand how this worked. You just put your whole family tree into your name. Tony extends this tradition by creating his own nicknames for people.

"Well, in one class that I taught up in the high school here, there were two Mary Catherine MacDonald's and the only way I could distinguish them… one was Mary Catherine Johnny Roddy Angus and the other was Mary Catherine Angus Jimmy Dan."

Apparently, it helps to throw in a geographical place name or two as well. Just for clarity.

"It might go back three generations. Johnny Billy Allan Cape North: This is John MacDonald, his father was Billy Allan and he came from Cape North. It's really very simple."

Tony's delivery was dry. Very dry. A Scot's wit sparkled beneath the gruff exterior, betrayed by a disarming accent of messy S's. Yesss. Yesss. Ach, well now… Let's look at the sometimes cruel nicknames, based on unhappy events. It's a good thing the Scots' humour includes a natural ability to laugh at one's self. (At least I hope that's true.) Tony told me about an embarrassing incident that marred one family's name for life.

"They were The Pickle Ass Petries. One of them was sitting on the top of a barrel of pickled herring in the company store in Lingan. He got in an argument and got squirming around and got wedged in the barrel. By the time they got him out, he was pickled."

And there are more name stories inspired by the same piece of anatomy:

"Proud Arse Rory was in Neil MacNeil's book, the *Highland Heart of Nova Scotia.* They had the first privy in the countryside so he was Proud Arse Rory What-Does-It-In-A-Box."

Tony never smiled during our entire conversation. He enjoyed the comic shock value while disguising his pastime as a pseudo-academic exercise. I wasn't fooled. He actually collected them for the fun of it. I was even sorry when the ones about the "ends" ended.

"Waterloo Dan MacDonald worked in the coal mines and when he came out to the wash house and got the black washed off, they could see, branded backwards across his buttocks, "Waterloo #2." Sometime when he was a little boy, he backed into the coal stove, the Waterloo stove, and was branded for life!" Ouch. The nickname stuck with him for life too! I would guess the coal stove also stuck to him for a moment. (Another Waterloo Dan, in Pictou County, was actually at the battle of Waterloo, as a boy piper. He also piped in the first train to Pictou County.)

But surely the playful Scots and Gaels must have incorporated body parts other than the derrière into their nicknaming system. I asked Tony about that and he told me the story of little Neily MacDonald. Young Neily lived on a farm and attended a one-room schoolhouse many years ago. One day the teacher was having a spelling bee. The students were all lined up at the front of the room. The teacher would ask one student to spell a word, then ask the next student to explain what it meant. The boy beside Neily got the word "quadruped." "Now Neily, what does that mean?' Tony said, mimicking the teacher. "Neily didn't know it anymore than if it was Japanese," said Tony. "But Neily's father was a school trustee and the teacher was staying at Neily's house, so she gave the lad a hint. 'I'll help you a little, Neily,'" Tony mimicked. "'What is it that I have two of and a cow has four of?'" The response from Neily, the naive farm lad, labelled him for life: Neily Tits MacDonald.

The Nova Scotia nickname phenomenon was celebrated in an October 1980 *Reader's Digest* article by David Big Christopher MacDonald. He lists some place name nicknames: Big Alex in the Woods, John Double Hill, Janie from the Brook, and Joe Meadow; and other miscellaneous handles: Sober Sandy (who often wasn't) and Hughie Tantum Ergo, who sang Latin hymns at benediction. Other hymn singers included two priests, one of whom worked as a print-shop apprentice before donning the collar. As a young man he was known as Alex the Devil. As a man of the cloth, he became Father Alex the Devil. The Most Reverend Malcolm MacEachern, over six-and-a-half-feet tall, was known by fellow bishops as the High Priest. Why not? It makes sense. It's a fine and proper pun that distinguishes between priests with like names. Big Christopher's *Digest* article also cites several occupation-induced nicknames: Allan Donald the Cobbler, Danny Donald the Piper, Allan White Blacksmith, and a family of MacMillans who have been the Dancer MacMillans since 1820.

Tony MacKenzie, not to be outdone by the Digest, told me about Donald the Mink of Baddeck, Cape Breton, who made moonshine. He hid his homemade hooch in holes along the riverbank. Ha! You can just picture him going from hole to hole, up to his knees, checking his wares. Mink indeed.

Tony insisted that nicknames were nothing to laugh at. To him, they are not nicknames at all. No, the Gaelic word for them is "sloinedh." It's a form of pedigree. Asking "What's your father's name?" is not comical, it's cultural. It's a traditional method of separating the Mc's from the Mac's. That can be a matter of life or death. At one time there were 640 MacDonald's working at the Dominion Steel and Coal Company in Cape Breton. More than 150 of them were John MacDonalds. The foreman needed some way to identify which MacDonalds were under-ground and which were safely above ground—especially in case of a serious bump. Those miners' names stuck outside the mineshaft. Take Donald MacDonald for example.

"He was hurt in the mine," said Tony, "and by the time they found him, his arms had set in the position of ten minutes to three. So, he was known as Donald the Clock."

"My father told me that one day there were five John MacDonalds in one car leaving the Legion Hall in Glace Bay. There was Jack Spud and Jack Flat and Johnny Billy Big Archie, Johnny Billy Allan Cape North and Johnny Angus Summer John. No one called them 'MacDonald.' I think Antigonish Jack and Jack Beefsteak were in the next car," Tony mused.

I love that. The Highland nicknaming system is wonderful. It helps put a name—or two—or three to a face, while giving vent to the Highland culture's special wit. This folksy fun with names adds meaning to the question, "What's your father's name?" in the Highland headquarters of Nova Scotia. Go ahead, ask. You may laugh a little… and learn a lot.

Raδio Roots
anδ Quiet Memories

*A nostalgic look at Nova Scotia's
pioneers of the airwaves.*

R adio.
The word has a powerful resonance. Like "schoolhouse" or "shoemaker," "radio" has its modern connotation but also suggests another era. Old-time radio is nostalgic. It's pre-war. It's images of grandparents, of big "staticky" wooden radio "sets," distant voices, old-style announcers enunciating with dramatic bravado. The image of the radio can transport us back in time, especially for those Nova Scotians, young and old, who cherish those former radio days. And they deserve to be cherished. Nova Scotia played a special role in the early days of radio. It might have to do with where we are.

Geographically, Nova Scotia sticks its nose into the Atlantic like a curious pooch tracking a scent. Our unique location has shaped our history and world connections in more ways than we realize. We are centrally positioned. We stand on the leading edge of the continent, poking our snouts into world commerce and communication. We are the historic in-betweens, betwixt Europe's powers and the great Boston States. Location, location, location! We have it. And it's helped us grow. We are a corner store at a busy intersection of world traffic. And we were the first to hear the earliest shouts from those busy streets.

The sounds of radio brought communication to a new level. It was the first technology to provide oral/aural communication to a mass audience. More than the printing press or even television, radio reached people's minds and imaginations in a way central to human experience. It magnified, expanded, and emphasized our oral tradition. Reaching the mind through the delicate ear, radio was the natural extension of a phenomenon which had its roots in primal villages—radio catapulted the spoken word to a new plane. That was exciting. It kept early radio pioneers up all night, tinkering and tapping, scanning and scoping—reaching into the airwaves for those faraway voices. Voices that made the hairs on the backs of their necks tingle. In the early days, radio was exhilarating.

John Joseph Fassett was one of our first radio communicators. He was a curious, inventive pioneer of our early airwaves. A genius with the relatively new technology called electricity, Joe Fassett loved radio. He was intrigued by its nuts and bolts—and its heart and soul.

Joe spent late nights in his small radio room in his house in the Dartmouth community of Woodside. The town of Dartmouth was the launching centre for "ham" radio activity in Nova Scotia back in 1913. Joe Fassett was our first licensed "ham" or amateur radio operator.

Joseph Fassett and daughter with old radio equipment on the stoop of 1923 Sugar Refinery Co. House.

He was also one of the first to intercept wireless radio messages from the sinking *Titanic* in the wee hours of April 15, 1912. He gained international recognition for relaying those distress messages to New York.

Fassett had emigrated from Kent, England before the turn of the twentieth century. Always fascinated by things electrical, he accepted work at the huge Acadia sugar refinery on the Dartmouth shore across from downtown Halifax. Joe was responsible for the electrical works at

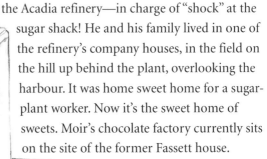

the Acadia refinery—in charge of "shock" at the sugar shack! He and his family lived in one of the refinery's company houses, in the field on the hill up behind the plant, overlooking the harbour. It was home sweet home for a sugar-plant worker. Now it's the sweet home of sweets. Moir's chocolate factory currently sits on the site of the former Fassett house.

Joe's imagination was sparked by the potential of the relatively new, intangible power of electricity. It was more than his work. It was his passion. A passion that kept him experimenting, inventing and communicating with the world in his spare time; worshipping the legacy of Morse and Marconi.

I first learned about Joe Fassett in a strange way. It was through another Nova Scotian who shared something in common with him. While Joe loved the unifying potential of radio communication, this other Nova Scotian hoped to unify the country with wood! This modern-day crusader for Canadian unity hoped to get his message out artistically. By building a tree. Not grow a tree, but *build* a tree—from scrap wood. He was collecting pieces of wood from Canadians, coast to coast. Each piece had to have a story or special meaning connected with it. He was sculpting a "Canadian Unity Tree." I suppose if Joe could build radios in the 1920s from glass tubes, wires and a battery, why not build a tree from scratch? Inventions come from daring to think differently.

Believe it or not, the tree builder's name was Mr. Aspin. While travelling in Canada's far west he happened to pick up a hitchhiker. He was, after all, collecting Canadian stories from ordinary folk. So the two got to talking. As a testament to the reach of Nova Scotia's tentacles, the hitchhiker had a Nova Scotia story. He was the great-grandson of Joe Fassett. His mother was Joe's daughter. Mr. Aspin mentioned this chance highway encounter in an interview on CBC Radio's *Maritime Noon*. That's how I found him. They asked him about *his tree*. I asked him about *history*. Radio history, that is.

Through Aspin, I tracked down Frances Sim, Joe Fassett's daughter who was living in Vancouver. She was happy to tell me about her father. Though she was in her eighties, she still referred to him sweetly as "'Daddy." Frances' voice was a little shaky but her feelings for her father were solid. She talked about his late-night sessions, tapping out Morse code messages. It took her back to when she was a little girl in the old company house behind the refinery.

"One of my most vivid memories is in the radio room—it was the front bedroom—watching Daddy at the key. He sat at a desk and I remember the key, and his finger going like mad. Daddy was always in the radio room. You know, I'd go to sleep listening to that thing: Dah-Dah-Dah, Dit, Dah-Dah, Dah-Dah."

Hearing Frances mimic the old sound sent chills up my spine. A sound from a bygone era, rich with nostalgia. Radio days. But the message that dash-and-dot carried, in the dark, early hours of April 15, 1912, must have chilled Joe Fassett to the bone. That night, he was the wireless operator on board the Canadian Government Ship *Minto*, the first of our Marine and Fisheries ships, in 1904, to be equipped with the wireless. Who received the SOS message from the *Titanic* and relayed it to New York authorities? Our boy Joe. The ship had struck an iceberg and was going down in the mid-Atlantic. When he died in 1956, the *New York Times* recognized Joe Fassett's efforts by publishing a tribute to him.

From ship life to shore life, Joe's love of radio had grown with the technology. He built and repaired radios for himself and for his friends. His daughter, Frances, remembers that Joe built a radio for her mother. And the hallway floor was always lined with radios he promised to fix in his spare time. For neighbours in the row of company houses who didn't have radios, Joe shared his new technological marvel.

"He had wires coming out from our house across the road," said Frances, "out into the field in front of the sugar refinery houses."

Those wires were Joe's radio antennae. He strung them out long to get better reception from longer distances. There were no radio stations in Nova Scotia as yet.

"When the fights were on, when anything important was on, he'd open the bedroom window and put the radio on the sill so everybody could hear it. Nobody else had radios, but Daddy did!"

The boxing matches were the most memorable early broadcasts that kept the neighbours' rapt attention. They would have heard the roar of the crowd in 1927 as Jack Dempsey, the "Manassa Mauler," went down in defeat to Gene Tunney. Those were the grand old days of early radio excitement. Imagine the cheers on the Fassett family's front lawn!

In 1919 a Marconi office opened on Granville Street in Halifax to sell radio parts. Marconi wireless stations had sprung up throughout North America. Amateurs everywhere were buying parts and learning to cobble together radio sets to listen to those sparky, "staticky," distant sounds on the Nova Scotia airwaves. My father, J. Clyde Nunn, was one of those radio amateurs in Sydney, Cape Breton. He tinkered with a brass radio key screwed to a small wooden board. He and his young friends also experimented with crystal radio sets. One of those friends told me that my father placed his radio set inside a metal washbasin, to capture more resonance from the weak sound. From that early radio exposure, my father went on to a career in broadcasting. Joe Fassett had that opportunity too. But he let it escape him.

The manager of the Marconi office eventually set up a radio station, CFCE, in the Marble Building on Barrington Street, over Phinney's Music Store. Although it was only temporary, CFCE was Nova Scotia's first official radio station that broadcast to the public. Using army radio telephone equipment, CFCE broadcast a series of musical tests to local amateur radio operators in 1922, the first music concert broadcast east of Montreal. Many radio buffs, Joe Fassett included, picked up the concert quite clearly. That same year, the first meeting of the Dartmouth Radio Club took place at the office of Cecil Zinck's funeral parlour, on Portland Street. Local radio buffs swapped advice on how to assemble radio parts, get good reception without interfering with each other's listening, and how to properly tune a set. Wilfred Stallard, a ninety-year-old Dartmouth resident, told me he remembered those radio club members at a garden party, trying to tune in New York stations on their radio sets.

Joe Fassett was granted the first amateur radio licence to broadcast in Nova Scotia in 1923. His call letters, "Canada 1-AR" were assigned by the Department of Marine and Fisheries. Radio was a revolutionary change for people, a marvellous novelty appreciated by many, but understood by few. Few had Joe Fassett's knowledge of the physics of radio. Not many had radios. It's a small wonder that his neighbours from the row of company houses crowded his front lawn to listen to the magical music and voices, even when the voice was Joe's own.

Apparently Joe and his wife, Annie, put on their own radio shows on Sundays. She played the old-style piano and he did the announcing. Or he would play

Joe Fassett received Ham radio cards from around the world.

gramophone music on his Ham transmitter, pretending the recorded artists were his own family. The Fassett family radio programs were broadcast from their living room. Joe did his announcing into a telephone receiver, which he used as a microphone. Frances told me about the role she played in helping her father during those early family performances.

"I can remember standing in our living room with this round thing hanging down from the ceiling. And I recited nursery rhymes while he changed the rolls on the piano."

Joe Fassett had invented the concept of "filling time"—a long-held tradition in broadcasting circles that is still practised by surprised announcers left hanging when equipment fails. Today we blame computer failure. Believe me, Joe, I've been there too. And without a blessed nursery rhyme to save me!

Joe decided against turning pro in the radio business. He preferred to broadcast out his living room window rather than try to make money at it. Apparently the treasurer of the Dartmouth Radio Club, Major W. C. Borrett asked Joe to join him in a new enterprise called commercial radio. He planned to open a station that would broadcast programs and sell air time to advertisers. But Joe was concerned about his family's future. He had children, one of whom was paralyzed from the waist down. Despite his love of radio, Joe couldn't risk his family's future on this commercial venture. If only he had known how it would pay off.

In 1926, W. C. Borrett, Cecil Landry, Lionel L. Shatford, and John Redmond opened Nova Scotia's first commercial radio station—CHNS. It opened in the Carlton Hotel in downtown Halifax and is still operating today. Many current Halifax broadcasters took their first on-air steps at that pioneer station. But Joe Fassett was not one of them. His friend, Major Borrett, became Colonel Borrett and went on to win broadcasting awards. His radio program, "Tales Told Under the Old Town Clock" featured historical Nova Scotian stories of ghosts, shipwrecks, and the lives of interesting folks around the province. They were later published in book form, adapted from his regular radio series. (Sound familiar?) But the point is, Borrett's gamble led to a long career in radio; one that Joe Fassett could have shared.

After the birth of CHNS, more radio stations began to pop up across the province. CJCB in Sydney, where my father began his radio career, started broadcasting on Valentine's Day, 1929. CBC Radio hit the airwaves from Halifax in 1936. CJFX Radio in Antigonish opened in March 1943 as an experiment in educational radio, a "University of the Air." St. Francis Xavier University started the venture, recruiting my dad to get it on the air and to manage the station. Later, more radio stations blossomed in Halifax and Dartmouth, on the south shore, in the Annapolis Valley, and in Yarmouth, Pictou County, Amherst, and Port Hawkesbury. Radio was everywhere! But Joe Fassett, radio pioneer, continued working at the sugar refinery and broadcasting to his neighbours on Sundays.

Despite his caution, Joe had a vision of radio's capabilities. He knew the technology inside out. His daughter described other radio-related inventions that Joe built. Somehow he made his own vacuum tube, long before they were readily available. He also built a six-inch glass tube that he plugged into a current and held against his daughter's jaw which helped ease the pain of her neuralgia. Frances remembered the contraption as a black box with six glass tubes in it. The one against her face had a ball shape at the bottom and a bluish-red light inside. She liked the warm feel of the tube against her skin and claims it cured her pain. Her father used a similar electrical invention to help his paralyzed son. The Fassett children were always aware that their father's gift was special. His genius with all things electrical led Joe to make a prediction that excited his oldest daughter, Frances, who loved the American radio programmes of the day.

"He had a vision of radio," said Frances. "I became interested in Buck Rogers when I got a little older. I couldn't wait for everything to be like it was on the Buck Rogers program. And Daddy told me that some day you will look at your radio and you'll see pictures! And that was a long time before anybody else said anything about it." A radio visionary predicting radio visuals. That was Nova Scotia's John Fassett.

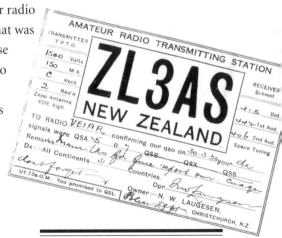

Joe Fassett's Ham radio reached as far
as New Zealand, that's a lot of ham!

A Hard Act to Follow

Evolution of a special vessel.

C ats have nine lives but they don't float well. Not like the mighty *Kipawo* ferry in Parrsboro. It's lived more lives than a cat—most of them at sea. The ferry's most recent incarnation is as a stationary stage for Ship's Company Theatre. It's a unique Nova Scotian theatre, worthy of artistic attention. This stage has had a very adventurous life. So, in case there are any visiting Broadway producers out there looking to resettle by the seashore, may I present *Kipawo*'s dramatic résumé:

Her name sounds Mi'kmaq but it was in fact derived from the first two letters of the three ports she was built to serve: Kingsport, Parrsboro, and Wolfville.

When she plied the waters of Minas Basin, she carried eight cars and up to 120 people.

When German trade vessels visited Minas Basin in the 1930s, their crews took photos of *Kipawo*'s loading technology.

The Germans copied *Kipawo*'s car sling, invented by her Nova Scotian crew, and used it to hoist their tanks and trucks from deck to dock during wartime invasions.

Kipawo was registered for use in the Canadian Navy under the incorrect name "Kipawa."

During World War Two, *Kipawo* patrolled the St. Lawrence River with a boarding party that stopped ships entering the Gulf area to check cargo and crews' papers.

This Nova Scotian ferryboat was fired upon by an enemy vessel. The torpedo slipped underneath *Kipawo*, missing her entirely.

After the war, a well-known Newfoundland family paid *Kipawo*'s captain one thousand dollars to declare her unseaworthy so she'd go up for public sale.

Kipawo was purchased to make the run between Portugal Cove and Bell Island, near St. John's.

She even transported Joey Smallwood as the radio character, "the Barrelman," on a tour of island outports.

While in Newfoundland, *Kipawo* caught fire and was purposely sunk (and later re-floated) to extinguish the flames. She also was run aground a few times.

An RCMP member from Parrsboro, stationed on the Rock, discovered the old ferry still existed, though unused and a little battered. A salvage effort failed when she sank again.

In 1982, a group from Wolfville and Parrsboro's nautical guru, Conrad Byers, arranged to have the Canadian Coast Guard tow the fifty-seven-year-old *Kipawo* home to Nova Scotia.

A welcoming ceremony greeted the old boat at Halifax Harbour.

Kipawo was eventually escorted to Parrsboro where she was converted into a high-and-dry drama house.

She is still supposed to be re-floated every eighteen months to maintain her legal register as a vessel, necessary for tax purposes.

The old ferryboat is beloved by many. Many couples fell in love on *Kipawo*. One couple even named their child "Kip."

When Fred Durant, *Kipawo*'s former captain, travelled from New Brunswick to visit the old boat, he asked to see her alone, to "talk to her one last time." Conrad Byers told me the captain died shortly after that visit. "He knew he was going. I guess that he felt *Kipawo* was a real person to him, a real living thing."

Indeed, she does live. *Kipawo* cheated death many times. Now she's sailing the uncharted waters of the theatre world. Her life was a drama, now drama is her life.

Selling Ship Shares by the Seashore

How Bluenose *played the numbers game her way.*

K now why the first *Bluenose* was special? No matter how fast she sailed, she stopped on a dime. Okay, that's just a fun pun. Actually it wasn't the dime that made *Bluenose* special. It was a pretty penny. That's what the racing schooner cost when first launched on the ocean waves in 1921.

So many investors clamoured to be *Bluenose* backers, a centuries-old nautical custom was corrupted to accommodate them all. The traditional selling of sixty-four shares—known as "the 64ths"—when launching a new vessel, was changed for *Bluenose*. Instead, 350 shares were sold at a hundred bucks apiece.

There's no such thing as a free launch.

The 64ths are mentioned as far back as medieval times. Thank you Rita Brown of the National Maritime Museum in Greenwich, England for that bit of info. In 1854, a British statute made the magic sixty-four share split compulsory.

Why?

Well, it's a number easily divided into quarters, eighths, and sixteenths. Ships get lost at sea. Sailors drown. Cargo sinks. Rum barrels disappear. Grown men cry. So it's better to spread the shares widely so no *one* shareholder loses his shirt with his ship. Thank Graham McBride, nautical historian in Halifax, for that depressing but practical explanation.

Here's another theory about the sixty-four shares, phoned in by an anonymous caller—probably a lawyer. He suggests that selling sixty-four shares was a tradition based on old English tax law. The tax on ships was 36 per cent of the ship's cargo. The ship's owner, captain, and crew shared the balance of the trip's bounty, 64 per cent. Hence sixty-fourths reared its easily divisible head. Other explanations for the sixty-four shares have been floated, but whatever the reason, the number has been carried on by the sheer force of tradition. That is, until *Bluenose* came along.

So, what's in a number?

A big, whopping, sailor's tradition, going back centuries, that's what. *Bluenose* shattered the sixty-fourths custom long before her hull hit water. A rebelliously good start for a spirited racing schooner that also shattered the hopes of her every competitor!

Bluenose herself was quite a number.

Beautiful *Bluenose*: for a vessel of the
seas, she sure broke a lot of ground.

A Tale of Two Floras

The Celtic connection of two Flora Macdonalds.

Speed bonny boat, like a bird on the wing,
"Onward," the sailors cry.
Carry the lad who's born to be king
Over the sea to Skye.
    Skye Boat Song, by Harold Bulton and Annie MacLeod, 1881.

C iamar a tha thu? That's my way of welcoming you to this story. It's Highland Scottish Gaelic, pronounced "kimmit ah ha ooh." It translates as "How are you?" Or, in Cape Breton, "How's she goin' buddy?" But this greeting needs no translation where Gaelic is still spoken in the Highland heart of Nova Scotia. In Antigonish and Pictou counties and on Cape Breton Island, Gaelic culture is like a Scottish Highlander's sword; steely strong and held with pride and loyalty to the blood of the clan. In northeastern Nova Scotia, Celtic descendants carefully preserve their bonds with the old country. That's why the mystique of Highland heroine Flora Macdonald still stirs hearts in this part of the world, two-and-a-half centuries after her death. But there's another reason why brave Flora's memory is cherished in Highland hearts. This stoic rescuer of the Scottish pretender to the British throne came to live in Nova Scotia. Why not? Doesn't

Bonnie Prince Charlie in Edinburgh.

every hero, heroine, inventor and genius come here, eventually? That's my theory and I'm sticking to it.

I received a short newspaper clipping about Flora's connection to Nova Scotia in the mail. It had a note attached:

Dear Mr. Know-It-All,

I'm a dedicated Information Morning addict. I'm also a fan of your series on odd or interesting stories about Nova Scotia or whatever.... The enclosed surfaced out of my paper-welter and it made me think of you. Is there a story here? Why would Flora and her husband stop over in Nova Scotia? I'll be listening.

Sincerely,

Paula Scott

Chester, Nova Scotia

Great Scot! A woman named Scott writing me about a woman who was a great Scot! It was a small irony, but I'll take irony in any dose. The question was also intriguing. Why indeed would the great heroine of Scottish mythology "stop over" in Nova Scotia? It wasn't on the way to Skye! The Flora Macdonald story has thrived over the centuries, recounted in ballads, poetry, literature, and oral tradition. In 1746, when the Scottish pretender to the throne, Bonnie Prince Charlie, was fleeing certain death at the hands of the British soldiers, this young woman of the Hebrides risked her life to save his. She whisked him off to the Isle of Skye. And Flora Macdonald ended up living a short time here in Nova Scotia. Some of her relatives are still here, some living, others dead. Yes, Paula, there is a story here. It exists as surely as the skirl of the pipes on Bobby Burns day.

The story begins with a linchpin event that would profoundly effect Nova Scotia's settlement as a colony—the bloody battle of Culloden in Scotland, April 16, 1746. It was the last battle of the "Forty-Five Rebellion," when the Scottish Jacobites were slaughtered—I mean defeated—by British forces. More than 250 years ago, forty minutes of fighting left a bitter legacy that still simmers in the blood of many Highland descendants. Young Charles Edward Stuart was bloodied and beaten after the Battle of Culloden. Fortunately, he ended up in Flora's capable hands.

You see, Charles represented the Jacobites, loyalists to the exiled James the Second. They wanted to restore the Stuart dynasty to the British throne. But William Augustus, the Duke of Cumberland, had a different idea: keep the status quo by killing the Scottish quota. Which he did. The Scottish Jacobites were badly outnumbered: Five thousand starving men against nine thousand well-fed ones. When the smoke cleared, the British forces had suffered about fifty casualties. The Jacobites lost about one thousand on the Culloden moor. In the ensuing weeks, another one thousand or so were tracked down and killed. In sportscaster parlance, that's known as a "rout." To this day, the flower called Sweet William—named for the conquering hero—is known in Scotland as a Stinking Willie or Sour Billy. But we all get along much better now. Don't we?

Nevertheless, the Culloden battle was a turning point for Nova Scotia. The insurrection was the last battle fought on Scottish soil. It helped lead to the destruction of the clan system. Sweet William took away the Highlanders' rights to wear kilts, wield weapons, and speak their own language. Threatened physically and culturally, many Scots were forced to seek a new life in New Scotland. They arrived in droves. (I think a drove is a small, wooden sailboat. Anyway, they got here.) The defeated leader of those courageous kilted underdogs, Bonnie Prince Charlie, escaped. Hunted and chased by William's militia, he took off with Flora in a boat.

Loud the winds roar, high the waves leap
Thunderclaps rend the air
Baffled, our foes stand on the shore
But follow they will not dare.

Now, this slice of Scottish history is not all serious, sad, and sombre. There's a little of the "silly" in there too. Legend says that Charlie, the fearless defender of his homeland, the bloodied, renegade hero, escaped with Flora in an open boat, disguised as her maid servant. He dressed like a woman—in a pretty petticoat and bonnet, perhaps? I suppose if he was used to the kilt and the tam, it wasn't much of a stretch. Charlie was given a special military pass listing him as Betty Burke, an Irish spinning maid. Ochh, 'twas a clever plan, sure! But think of the irony. The great warrior, pretender to the throne of one of the world's leading powers, wrapped in a frilly frock and answering to the name "Betty the spinner." I apologize, but I find that funny. I'm sure the prince laughed at himself—much later. He probably didn't laugh much during the boat ride. Yet good Flora showed strong nerve and provided soft comfort to her frilly, fugitive prince on those dangerous waters.

Though the waves leap, soft shall ye sleep
Ocean's a royal bed
Rocked in the deep, Flora will keep
Watch by your weary head.

Flora kept careful watch. And the disguise worked. Flora Macdonald, under a hail of gunfire at one point, spirited the lad who was "born to be king, over the sea to Skye." The prince was forced to leave behind his beloved homeland, with only memories of his many men, slaughtered on the moor.

Many's the lad fought on that day
Well the claymores could yield
When the night came silently lay
Dead on Culloden's field.

When Flora was questioned by the militia she told them she was going to Skye to visit her mother. The British have a soft spot for Mums so they bought it. Flora's acting skills saved Bonnie Prince Charlie's neck. He fled to France, with hopes of one day returning to fight again for his claim to the British crown.

Burned are our homes, exile and death
Scatter the loyal men
Yet ere the sword cool in the sheath
Charlie will come again.

History did not oblige the sentiments of the Skye boat song. Charlie did not come again. But the legacy of his foolhardy or fearless fight survived the centuries, as does the legacy of his foolproof yet frilly flight. Flora paid for her loyalty with a short imprisonment in the Tower of London, then was sent home to Scotland in 1746. Flora's legacy is still alive in Highland hearts here in Nova Scotia, and particularly in the heart of the Honourable Flora MacDonald (capital "D") from North Sydney, Nova Scotia. This Flora was a feisty member of Canada's Parliament during the 1970s and 80s. She served under two prime ministers, Joe Clark and Brian Mulroney. At different times, she held the offices of Secretary of State for External Affairs, Employment and Immigration Minister, and Minister of Communications. She proved to be tough, much like her Scottish namesake. I called her up, out of the blue. It was just a lucky guess that this once politically powerful Flora from Cape Breton would have something to say about Flora the Hebridean heroine. I hit the jackpot.

Flora MacDonald is past retirement age but still working hard in Ottawa. I reached her at her home and learned that she and the historical Flora share a lot more than just the name. Today's Flora MacDonald has eight biographies of her heroic namesake, along with lots of other Flora Macdonald collectibles.

"I have four paintings that were done of her. Some of them show her greeting the prince when she first met him. And photographs from Kilmuir, on the Isle of Skye, where she is buried. They come from various people. They have also sent me packets of Flora Macdonald (sewing) needles. I have a very small, lovely metal reproduction of Flora Macdonald mounted on top of a thimble. And it is named in honour of Flora Macdonald."

Now, that is special; Flora's collection of Flora. Obviously, the modern-day Flora identifies closely with the Flora of old. Her grandfather and her father searched diligently to find a genealogical connection between Flora's family and the historical Flora. They came up empty. That's not to say it's not there. Any Nova Scotian knows that those MacDonald family trees have far-reaching branches and deep roots. Any blood connection is possible if you look long enough. Flora told me she does look like the heroic Flora. They share the same Celtic facial features. I think they also share a certain steeliness of character. Backbone. It took courage to do what our Floras did. Flora respects that in her namesake.

"Of course she wanted him to escape, but to go with this strange company in a small boat, from the outer islands, at night, as they say, 'over the sea to Skye,' would be pretty daunting to a young woman.

However, she carried it out bravely and there's lots of songs and stories about that."

I was not the only one to make the Flora/Flora connection. In 1996, the Flora Macdonald College for young women in North Carolina invited our Nova Scotian Flora to speak to faculty and students on the 250th anniversary year of the Battle of Culloden. Why is there a Flora Macdonald College in North Carolina? Well, therein lies the reason the historic Flora Macdonald, small "d," arrived in Nova Scotia. In fact, wasn't that the information that our letter writer was asking for? (Go ahead, check. I'll wait.)

In 1750, Flora married a future Highland military captain, Allan Macdonald. Shortly after, like many Scots, they emigrated to North Carolina. Then, the American War of Independence broke out. Flora's husband was appointed brigadier-general by the governor. Both Allan and Flora had taken an oath to the British king, so in the American Revolution they were loyal to the same throne against which Flora had conspired with Bonnie Prince Charlie. Colonial politics makes strange bedfellows. The two-way tug on the heroic Flora's allegiances is nicely reflected in the title of one book in Flora MacDonald's collection in Ottawa; *Flora Macdonald: The Most Loyal Rebel.* I think that describes both women. Dedicated but independent. In fact Flora of old showed great loyalty during the American rebellion. Always an active woman in manly affairs, Flora helped Allan raise troops. She accompanied her husband in his campaigns until he was captured along with the couple's two sons, Charles and Alexander.

Allan Macdonald and his sons were held as prisoners of war until the Americans won the day. When released in August 1778, Allan came to Halifax, Nova Scotia, to serve in the Royal Highland Emigrant Regiment.

Map of Skye.

Flora couldn't join her husband in Nova Scotia right away. She was detained by American soldiers but eventually released. Lucky her, she joined Allan just in time to experience the bitterly cold Nova Scotia winter of 1778–79. Flora was fifty-six. She and Allan and their sons, shivered through those cold months at Fort Edward in Windsor. Allan was commander of the small fort. One winter here was enough for Flora. She returned home to balmy Kingsburgh, Scotland. Her husband followed her home, five years later, giving up a chance to settle on a land grant in Nova Scotia. We might *translate* it as "New Scotland" but apparently there's still no place like home. Flora and Allan lived out their days in the old country, where she died on March 5, 1790. She was

buried, wrapped in a sheet that her prince had once slept in while in hiding on Skye.

As for that other Flora MacDonald, in our nation's capital, well she also waged a few wars of her own. A strong woman among men, she joined many tough campaigns—and weathered some chilly years on the opposition side. I pondered these parallels after Ms. MacDonald and I spoke. I mused about how

Parliament Buildings, Ottawa.

far Flora MacDonald might have gone in modelling her life after her heroine. Would she, for instance, have dressed Bonnie Prince Mulroney in a petticoat and bonnet to smuggle him over the troubled waters of free trade? Hmmm. She would have had to take him further than the Isle of Skye to save his political career. Perhaps, in this tale of two Floras, the comparison stops there.

Culloden addendum:
A Mystical Memorial

Flora MacDonald's personal collection is not the only memorial to the Culloden legacy in Nova Scotia. The most public reminder we have of the Culloden disaster is a stoic stone cairn erected over the remains of three Scottish settlers. It stands in Knoydart, on the water's edge, near the Pictou-Antigonish county line. This monument marks the final resting place of three Bonnie Prince Charlie supporters, survivors of his historic uprising. Like many other Scots forced to leave their homeland, they settled in Nova Scotia, had families and died here.

Their cairn stands tall on a cold bluff, overlooking the Northumberland Strait. It is reached by a winding wooded trail leading from roadside to seashore. The trail leads back two and a half centuries, and hundreds of Nova Scotian Scottish descendants make this trip through time every April. They honour the anniversary of the Culloden killing with a poignant ritual by the cairn; they remember the dead, and those who survived to settle our shores.

Catherine Anderson in Avondale, Pictou County, is a direct descendant of one of those veterans of the bloody Culloden defeat. Every April she respects their history and honours their memory. She feels an ancient

The cairn that marks the graves of three Culloden warriors in Pictou County.

heartache, as if the tragedy of their clan was fresh. There was loss of life but not of tradition. Strength in clan culture keeps her ancestors' memories alive. So does the annual walk through that symbolic trail in the woods. For Catherine, it's a trip back in time.

She described the ritual to me: "At a few minutes before eleven we gather at the roadside. I pick out the flag bearers who are descendants of these men and they have the flag of Nova Scotia, the Canadian flag, the Scottish flag, and the Glenfinnan flag (named for the place where Prince Charlie first planted his flag of insurrection on Scottish soil). They follow the pipers, then the flag bearers, then the people in all the colours of their kilts; the Frasers, the MacIntoshes, the MacDonalds, all walking down."

The Celtic flavour of the gathering grows stronger as you reach the towering cairn on the hillside, with the ocean stretching out beneath it. Erected in 1938 by local people, the cairn was built of common field-stone, a few taken for nostalgia's sake, from the Culloden battlefield itself. The symbolism of this stone cenotaph is as thick as the stones themselves. These stones touch hearts. The ceremony is rich with meaning, emotion, and memory. Four sentinels in kilts surround the tall marker. Everyone forms a circle. The bagpipes play. The pipes' lament fills the cool April air and warms the Highland hearts, then wafts away over the waves.

"And then we begin with prayers," said Catherine. "Prayers said in Gaelic and English. Not only for those who lie buried at Knoydart, but all those who fought at Culloden. Prince Stuart supporters as well as the king's Hanoverian supporters. We don't leave them out, because they were Scottish too."

Blood against blood. A people divided by power. But those Scots who fought for their choice of king, fought with heart and soul. The inscription on the stone cairn pays tribute to their passionate loyalty to their pretender to the throne, Bonnie Prince Charlie:

Let them tear out our bleeding bosoms,
Let them drain our dearest veins
In our hearts is Charlie, Charlie
While a drop of blood remains.

Two of the Culloden survivors buried beneath that inscription are John MacPherson and Hugh MacDonald. The third is Angus MacDonald, Catherine Anderson's great-great-great-great-grandfather. The monument and the moment are deeply personal for her. Catherine believes, as do many, that that battle lead to the sharp rise in Nova Scotia's Scottish immigrant population.

"Although we lost the battle, it was the last battle fought on Scottish soil. And the defeat had very bad results for the Highlanders, as they lost their rights to their traditional weapons, their dress, and their language. It changed forever their life in the Highlands. It changed the clan system. This defeat was the first of events that lead to the settlement of eastern mainland Nova Scotia. It's the pioneer cemetery."

Whether this defeat was in fact the first, or the worst, it's certainly come to represent events that pushed Scots from their home to our shores. Catherine's voice is clear and soft as she speaks of Culloden. She feels this history inside her.

"It makes your blood run cold. It's very sombre. It has great feeling. We do it in tribute to these ancestors who made us what we are. We feel that we are part of it all."

It's the circle of Scottish life—commemorating death to celebrate life. Catherine has been to the Culloden battlefield, in search of spirits of long-gone relatives, to give life to names on her family tree. She's walked on the moor. She saw the cairn in the Culloden cemetery. The Nova Scotia stone memorial looks very similar. That gave her a "very strong feeling," one that moved Catherine to pick up a few small stones from that place where her ancestor, Angus MacDonald, risked his life for his beliefs. He was one of few lucky ones who survived. Family links stayed strong. For so long. Catherine brought her treasures home to keep in a drawer, just to "feel part of it all."

The World Calls Canso

*An historic place of codfish
and cables coming ashore.*

C anso, Nova Scotia is a tiny, troubled town that might remind
you of an answering machine message.
"Sorry. There's no one here to take your call right now... "
It's sad but true. Since the fishery faded, Cansoites are fighting
extinction. But long ago, when there were plenty of fish in the sea, there
was always someone in Canso to take a message. The Canso area
became Canada's Communication Central. Heck, the information
highway was born there—well its grandfather was, anyway.

Let's trace Canso's techno-trend. The first trans-Atlantic cables
between Canada and Great Britain, came ashore in that area; the first, at
nearby Tor Bay in 1874; the next, at Canso proper in 1881. (Newfoundland wasn't part of Canada as yet, so its early cables don't count. They
can't claim Cabot either, but they do.) Three years later, another cable
came ashore at Fox Island, off the Canso coast. The relay station for that
cable was at Hazel Hill. Nearby, at Little Dover, a relay cable stretched off
to New York.

The first Canso cable was almost five inches thick. Its copper core
was wrapped in a lead armour, protecting it from icebergs and anchors.
The cable was spooled off the back of a huge cable ship, forming one
continuous cord, across the ocean floor. A slow process. I wonder if
Canso folks stayed home the whole day waiting for the cable guy?

The original trans-Atlantic cable is still celebrated at Bill
MacMillan's campground. He works with the Canso Historical Society.
Bill told me how Morse Code "sparks" were read in a dark room,
translated, and then relayed over telegraph lines—also a slow process.
That's why a young Western Union employee in Canso invented a
forerunner to the teletype machine. Queens County native, Fred Creed,

created the high-speed automatic printing system in 1889. The word spread fast, in more ways than one.

"By about 1913, his new system was being used regularly," Bill said, "to transmit the London newspapers to all the major centres in Great Britain and Europe." From telegraph to teletype to publishing. Canso's techno-trend evolved.

"It's an interesting sequel to the story that we've now got a local POP (point of presence) site on the Internet," Bill boasted. Now people across the country can read about the old cable on the town's World Wide Web site. Canso connecting with Canada, again!

Recently a new communication link came to tiny Canso, offering fresh hope for the town since its decline. The first annual Stan Rogers Folk Festival in 1997 attracted a crowd bigger than Canso's population. I loved every minute of it. The festival was a musical message from a steadfast community, translated: "We're not dead yet."

Canso is beautiful, historical, and now musical. You should pay a visit. Bring your tent and camp out on the site of Canada's first message centre.

Go Fish

Proof that Nova Scotia tuna tastes as good with money as it does with mayo.

*C*anada's Ocean Playground. According to the slogan on our licence plates, Nova Scotia is a fine place to play. The rich and famous of long ago certainly knew that. A flotilla of them floated here in the first half of the century to have a barrel of fun reeling in tons of tuna.

Big wigs after big fish! It was *the* thing to do if you were wealthy, powerful—and bored.

Picture Al Capone's enforcer, the chairman of the board of the Chicago Mafia syndicate, casting his line overboard on a sunny Nova

Scotia morning in 1922. The brutal Tony Accardo actually fished here. He was a ruthless extortionist, murderer, and loan shark. A loan shark who loved tuna.

"His nickname was 'Big Tuna' because he fished tuna off Wedgeport," Cyrille LeBlanc told me. Cyrille is—get this—President of the Wedgeport Sport Tuna Fishing Museum and Interpretive Centre. (It's a long title, but you should see the one that got away.) Cyrille told me that Accardo "was also called 'Joe Batters' because that is how he would settle accounts for Al Capone." Let's hope he used a rod for the tuna (although I do like battered fish).

President FDR also fished off Shelburne, Liverpool, and Wedgeport. Roosevelt brought along his tackle box, fishing hat, a coast guard cruiser, and a US destroyer. Sounds like he was *hunting* tuna.

"That was quite impressive," said Cyrille, "Children at that time visited him in his Savannah sailing yacht." FDR even had a separate coast guard patrol schooner for the media. Hmmm, a press gang at sea.

While that famous fisher came from the oval office, another came from the square ring. Years after Gene Tunney's tenth-round defeat of Jack Dempsey in 1927, he caught tuna off Nova Scotia. Why not? He was a boxer with a good hook. And he reeled in a heavy-weight fish that tipped the scales at 608 pounds.

A huge tuna hoisted to the Wedgeport dock. How *do* they get them in those small round cans?

This boxing champ was quite a catch himself, according to some Wedgeport women. Tunney, however, was impressed by the massive hands on his guide, Nova Scotia's George

Leblanc. "Boy, if I had your hands, I'd never lose a fight the rest of my life," said the boxer to the fisherman. I'll bet the tuna has similar vengeful thoughts toward his pursuers. "If only I had fists.... "

How about ranch hands? Western novelist Zane Gray rounded up wild tuna here, as did, of course, the man's man, Ernest Hemingway. Washer and dryer magnate Robert Maytag was so lonely he came here to befriend fish. And hockey legend Jean Beliveau got fifty-five minutes for hooking. That's not a penalty, that's a record. That's how long it took Beliveau to score an eight-hundred-pound fish. Gosh, oh golly, what a great play! Let's roll that back for a second look!

Wedgeport's wharf not only attracted male VIP fishers. Picture the so-called First Lady of radio, singer Kate Smith, dangling her bare toes and a fishing line off that pier. God Bless America.

An "Ocean Playground"? Well, the big kids sure had fun playing Catch the Tuna, way back when. These days the fish are fewer and the sport is serious business.

Would "Canada's Ocean Battleground" fit on a licence plate?

Everybody Must Get Sconed

A special sample of Scotland's historic Stone of Scone.

I'll bet you can't say you've inspired an international jewelry exhibit, can you? I didn't think so. That's just one of many benefits of being a radio storyteller with a ridiculous title, hokey theme music, and a willing straight man. My own peculiar brand of historical journalism once crossed paths with the talents of a Nova Scotian artist. Our meeting motivated him artistically. Me? I got a great story out of it. A story that spans from biblical times to the present day, with stops in

Scotland, the Arctic Circle and Mahone Bay, Lunenburg County. Gather round. I'll begin at the beginning.

Seven hundred years ago…. Wait, that might not be the exact beginning. Hold that thought. First, fast forward to 1996. It's a cool Friday evening in November. I'm at an art opening in Studio 21, a vibrant downtown gallery in the city of Halifax. Amid the free wine and cheese (there are some paintings too), I meet a Nova Scotian jewelry artist. Orland Larson is shortish, with wispy grey hair and eyes that grin. He speaks with enthusiasm.

"I was going to write to you today," he proclaims. "I have some pieces of the famous Stone of Scone that's been all over the news this week!" Bells go off in my head. "Great story!" they clang. But my mouth says quietly, "Hmm, that's interesting. Please, tell me more."

Now we can go back. Seven hundred years ago the ancient, traditional Stone of Scone (some say "skone," some say "skoon"—let's call the whole thing rock) was taken from Scotland as war booty by the English King, Edward I. It was this symbolic rock upon which the Scots had once crowned their kings—a coronation stone. Scottish legend has it that the rock was found in the Holy Land and served as Jacob's pillow in biblical times. Hence its nickname, Stone of Destiny. Some say it was a meteorite that crashed to earth. Others believe that the special stone was confiscated from the Holy Land during the crusades. It arrived in Ireland in 700 BC. (Don't worry, I'm working my way around to a proper beginning.) The Irish, you see, took the deadweight to Scotland when they invaded that country in the ninth century. And upon that rock, the Scottish crowned their kings. Have I left anyone out? Let's see, the Holy Land, Ireland, Scotland. This rock was quite a land rover. But seven hundred years ago it was moved again, as I said, to England. Just how this heavy rock was lugged from place to place, I can't tell you. This chunk of mother earth is a rough-hewn block of greyish-black sandstone. It's about eleven inches high, two feet wide, and weighs over three hundred pounds. It's heavy and awkward to budge; it's no rolling stone. (Although it had a world tour that would make Mick and Keith jealous. And it's almost as old as they are.)

When King Edward I captured the Stone of Scone, in 1296, the symbolism of his actions was powerful. This revered rock-of-ages came to represent English domination over Scotland. Yet to the Scots it had long been their centuries-old icon of sovereignty and freedom. Its loss was devastating. The English stashed the stone in Westminster Abbey, where they stash their kings and queens. The special Scottish stone sat under the seat of the English coronation chair for seven hundred years (which brings us to the present). The Stone of Scone was formally returned to Scotland on November 15, 1996. Since it was an election year, the rock's return was a political offering of sorts. But the stone still remains the property of the Queen and must be brought back to London for coronations. Nevertheless, its royal transfer to Scotland was accompanied by much pomp and ceremony. The stone was escorted by guards on the 640-kilometre journey north to the border village of Coldstream, on Scotland's Tweed River. A bagpiper musically escorted the stone to the centre of the bridge where there was a toast of whiskey for both the piper and the cabinet minister responsible for Scotland, commemorating the historical transfer. (Or maybe he was there for the whiskey. A little scotch on the rock.) At any rate, from Coldstream, Scottish soldiers escorted the stone to Edinburgh. But before the rock was put on display in Edinburgh's hilltop castle, conservationists checked it over to see if it needed repairs. (Make note of that. History repeats itself here.) Stone stories crisscrossed the world on national newscasts and made headlines everywhere. "Stone of Scone Returns Home." "After 700 Year Wait, Scots Welcome Stone of Scone Return." These newscasts and headlines were what the jewelry artist, Orland Larson, had mentioned when we chatted at the art gallery in Halifax. All of the above was fresh in my mind from the previous week's media coverage. That is to say, I tried to sound like I knew what I was talking about.

I asked Orland how he managed to get these valuable pieces of this ancient yet currently topical hunk of sandstone. Therein lies another twisted tale. And more globetrotting. Even some for me. I, of course, wanted to see Orland's valuable chunks of this special stone and find out how they landed in his hands. We agreed to meet at his old house in Mahone Bay, Lunenburg County, where he has a small jewelry studio. Snow glimmered in bright sunlight on the frigid day I drove down the highway. The roads were a little slick but I arrived in one piece, and crunched my way across the frozen yard to Orland's turn-of-the-century house, overlooking the bay. Over an hospitable bowl of soup, the jeweller and the journalist shared a story. Orland described how samples of the royal rock came to be in his possession.

Hang on now, we have to back up. Just a little. Forty-some years before, the Stone of Scone went missing from its usual place in England's Westminster Abbey. It was stolen on Christmas Day, 1950. It had been smuggled back to Scotland by Scottish nationalists who were Glasgow University students. The theft is part of recorded history. As a young art student in London during the 50s, Orland often visited Westminster Abbey, so he's tickled at being a part of the stone story. As Orland explained, the Scottish students smuggled the precious stone from the old Abbey under the cover of darkness and whisked it back to Scotland in the back seat of a car. But something went wrong.

"They gave it to a certain man [William White]," Orland explained, "who was thrilled that the stone had come back to Scotland and promised he would guard it with his life." Or maybe he would guard it with his wife. Sorry, I can't read my soup-stained notes. No, I'm sure it reads "with his life." Anyway, the man was William White, another Scottish nationalist. "Unfortunately, it had been broken in the move," said Orland, "so he got a stone mason to repair it." Something always gets broken when you move. But in this case it was a two- or three-thousand-year-old stone that meant a lot to lots of people. Not good. The skilled stone mason, Bertie Grey, made the repair but apparently he bit off more than he could glue. He gave the stone and the leftover bits and pieces to Mr. White since he couldn't rebuild the broken rock to its original heft. A royal stone gathers no mass.

Orland the jeweller first learned about the emergency repairs to the Stone of Scone in his previous life as an art educator. (A cold one. He was teaching in the Canadian Arctic in 1962.) There, on Broughton Island, off the east coast of Baffin Island, he met John Macdonald, a Hudson's Bay manager. One evening they were talking about the Stone of Scone's theft, when John surprised Orland by giving him the remnants of that same stone. John had inherited the rock pieces from his father, William, who was once friends with William White, the patriotic Scotsman who had secretly harboured the stolen stone. The jeweller in Orland responded with great glee. These remnants were precious pieces of posterity. Gems and stones are germane to a jeweller's life. Orland was deeply touched and wanted to show his gratitude.

Orland told his northern buddy, John, that he would make a pendant for John's mother from a piece of the sandstone gift, which he did.

Orland confided that John's Scottish mum wore Orland's handiwork around her neck proudly, with an air of defiance. The stone of scorn.

Now, that's a convoluted tale. Frankly, I was confused. Perhaps you are too. I asked Orland to tell me the story again, slowly. You almost need a play-by-play description to keep track. Actually, on reflection, that's what this rock's rocky road reminds me of, a rebounding puck that everyone wants a piece of. Perhaps a Danny Gallivan-esque play-by-play would help:

The stone is snatched. It's smuggled across the line into Scotland. The rock is dropped. Whoops! It breaks. A stone mason repairs it. Some pieces stay behind the line. A Scottish nationalist hides it. He pockets the pieces. The nationalist passes them to William Macdonald. It's Macdonald over to his son, John, who moves to the high Arctic. Lots of open ice around him. He takes his time. He passes the pieces to the jeweller, number six, Orland Larson. Larson takes possession. He fashions a stone pendant for Macdonald's mother. Then he pockets some pieces! Perfect. A Scottish Spin-o-rama! The crowd goes wild!

Well, our soup bowls were empty. The sky was grey through the frosted glass of Orland's kitchen window. The temperature dropped. Must be getting back soon or my car will be skating and I'd be offside. The big moment had arrived. I had the story, now I was finally about to see these ancient chunks of Scottish history… to touch them; to feel the richness of their heritage in my hands. I was excited. Orland and I went into his crowded little studio. He went to his workbench to collect the precious stone samples. This is what followed:

> Orland: "I have about a tablesp… a teaspoon, a good teaspoon of the granules."
>
> Me: (Incredulous) "You have granules?"
>
> Orland: "Er, well, ah, there was never more than little bits and pieces or chips… it's not… it wasn't a large piece off the stone. It's just the filings, as it were, when the repair was being made."
>
> Me: (Incredulouser) "Filings?"
>
> Orland: "Yeah, well, of the stone."
>
> Me: "Of the stone! I drove an hour to Mahone Bay to see dust?"
>
> Orland: "Ahhh… "

This was pathetic. Here I was, shivering in a cold room, a long, dangerous drive ahead, holding dust. Was this how great journalistic investigators started out? Not bloody likely. Orland tried to make up by saying that my interest in his dust had inspired him to create an international art exhibit. Orland *is* a jeweller with a reputation—he founded the Jewelry Department at the respected Nova Scotia College of Art and Design in the 1970s. He tried to distract me by describing his great exhibit idea. Nine meaningful objects in nine small, ornate glass bottles, each having a different theme. He planned to show them across Canada and possibly in Europe. The Nova Scotia Know-It-All exhibit! No, I won't be inside one of those tiny glass vials. I have work to do. Orland stressed that it was my curiosity about his stone saga that motivated him to share his vial of ancient dust and his other bottled collector's items with the world. "Okay," I said, "I'll accept that." The trip wasn't a complete waste. I began to feel better. In fact, I was becoming intrigued with that delicate bottle of meaningful dust. It was, after all, going to be the highlight of an international show. I looked at the filings in their tiny glass container; a delicate, antique Nova Scotia ink bottle made of clear glass, with a narrow neck. Orland had fastened a tiny silver crown around the bottle's little cork. "It looks insignificant," he reasoned. "But it is extremely significant to me and to Scots."

He handed me the symbolic sample. It was tiny. The filings looked like pepper! I felt ridiculous but I acquiesced. I examined the vial. Ever so carefully, I tweaked off the cork. With a tiny tip and tap, I poured a few granules into my palm. Wow. Scottish Stone of Skoon dust! I paused. Nothing yet. Hmmm, slowly a realization dawned as minuscule as the sample I was holding. It was part of an historic, world-wide saga of power, politics, invasion, thievery, sentiment, negotiation, family connections, and artistic endeavour. Scone or skoon, this powder had power! And it's right here in Nova Scotia. God bless Orland Larson for holding tight to those historic black bits.

As for the jewelry exhibit, I'm honoured. But I may never look at my pepper shaker in quite the same way again.

The Patronage King

The man who invented the give-and-take of Nova Scotia politics.

Our fisheries may be in decline but we can rely on one Nova Scotian resource that shows no sign of running dry: patronage. Let's face it. Politically speaking, it's a centuries-old Nova Scotia tradition. And it probably has a bright future ahead.

One of our early premiers honed political patronage to an art form. Michael Wallace was a colonial administrator in the early 1800s. He was the king of patronage. In fact, he was known as King Michael. Dr. David Sutherland, an historian in Halifax, told me that King Michael had a firm grip on the pork barrel. "He controlled everything. Our first dollars were called 'Michael Wallaces' because they bore his signature."

King Michael liked the power of his office a bit too much. No, he *loved* the power—a lot.

"If you wanted anything," said Dr. Sutherland, "from land grants to requests for relief, you had to knock on his door and smile nicely. If he didn't like you he had a great repertoire of four-letter words."

I got the impression from Dr. Sutherland that Michael Wallace was not very nice. One press account seems to bear that out. I love this quote from the old *Colonial Patriot* newspaper, describing Michael Wallace: "A mind perpetually boiling with the effervescence of irritation." It's enough to give patronage a bad name! He certainly gave Port Wallace a bad name—his own. Port Wallace is part of an historic series of locks that once connected Halifax Harbour with the Bay of Fundy. Someone thought naming it after King Michael might buy some favour. But later on, some mapmakers began spelling it "W-a-l-l-i-s." It was pronounced the same, but it had a better reputation. Dr. Sutherland explained that Admiral Sir Provo Wallis was in the famous battle between the *Shannon* and the *Chesapeake*, when the British (including Nova Scotians), captured an American warship off the coast of Boston." That Wallis had a much cooler image.

It's true, Nova Scotia's patronage pool is old and deep. King Michael helped to dig it, then was first to plunge right in. Many others jumped in after him. I wonder who'll be poised next on the diving board.

Communist Insurrection in Amherst

A Nova Scotian saves Leon Trotsky's life.

L ooking across the desk into the steely eyes of a left-wing socialist agitator made the Nova Scotian interrogator nervous. A novice backbencher facing Alexa McDonough? No, it was an Amherst man facing Leon Trotsky.

Captain Carmen Wightman felt the fury of the infamous revolutionary's glare. Wightman was questioning Trotsky in Amherst's old iron foundry, converted into a prisoner of war camp.

It was April 1917.

Trotsky's ship had been intercepted on its way to Russia from New York. He was headed home to join the Bolshevik revolution. But naval authorities were worried that the revolutionaries would deflect Russia's war effort, so Mr. T and family were detained at Halifax. His wife and two sons were sent to stay with the Horowitz family, on Market Street, near the present site of the Scotia Square mall.

Leon was taken briefly to the Citadel then was jailed with Germans at the POW camp in Amherst. Captain Wightman, later a major and mayor of the town, risked only brief glimpses into his prisoner's powerful gaze. Wightman described Trotsky's mesmerizing glare to Peter Latta, historian, and his next-door neighbour. Latta told me what Captain Wightman told him.

"He said that Trotsky had one of the most intense gazes he had ever encountered. He said that when Trotsky looked at you it was as though his eyes were daggers stabbing through you."

Peter Latta described how Trotsky and Wightman squared off.

"They got into a heated argument. Trotsky lunged at Wightman. The guard, a Private Buck, nearly ran Trotsky through with his bayonet."

But Captain Wightman intercepted the soldier and made Buck back off. An Amherst man saved Leon Trotsky's life on Nova Scotia soil! Now *there's* a twist in the communist plot. Trotsky was held illegally for a few weeks before being released. Upon returning to Germany, he immediately joined Lenin to further the revolution that had just broken out. Ah, the communist fish that got away! Later, Captain Wightman was speechless. He realized the man whose life he saved went on to paint Russia red.

Wightman might have guessed Mr. Trotsky would incite the masses. During his short prison term here, the commanding communist frequently translated the Halifax *Chronicle-Herald* newspaper for a group of German prisoners. His dynamic presence at the Amherst prison camp kept the guards on their toes. Trotsky's powerful persona could stir a crowd to trouble in a flash. After a few weeks, our military brass realized they could no longer hold the revolutionary against his will without legal cause. He was not a prisoner of war. Trotsky was released with his family and sent home. What followed were years of communist persecution, during which his people lived desperate lives under the heavy boot of an abusive state. All of that might not have happened, if one moment in Nova Scotia's history had been different.

Leon Trotsky.

Hickory Dickory Dock, the Man Who Lived in Our Clock

A timely tour inside the Halifax Town Clock.

Bing, Bong, Bing. BONG!
The Town Clock on Citadel Hill in Halifax is a shiny postcard that chimes. Stripped of its function as timekeeper for the old garrison town of Halifax, this clock is in future time. It's not 1803 anymore. Today, the clock tower belongs to the tourists. Its job is to be photogenic. Quaint. Charming. Ye olde towne clocke. In many slick and quick promo spots, this clock *is* Nova Scotia. For three seconds. Instant recognition. Symbolism on the hillside. Is it really possible anymore to see the essence of the clock's character? Its true clockiness? Can we get beneath the touristy trappings of this timely icon, beyond the million postcards, images, lapel pins, and plastic placemats? I'd like to think so.

My approach to breaking the icon barrier is to find a way around it, to get into its clockworks, figuratively speaking, from the inside out. But in this case, I'm speaking literally. True, some colleagues at CBC Radio were skeptical when I told them I'd met someone who used to live inside the town clock. I didn't blame them. After all, they'd never heard of the family that lived in the clock (or any clock for that matter), and they work just over the hill. Citadel Hill, that is. A phone call came to our answering machine about some other topic and the caller mentioned the clock family as an aside. Again, proof that good radio comes from the listeners. That's how I came to meet clock-dweller, Dennis Gill.

Dennis told me about his childhood. In the 1960s, his father worked for the parks service as a caretaker of the historic tick-tock tourist attraction. He lived inside the clock with his young family. Many promotional photos show that the clock tower sits on a rather large square wooden base. It's actually a good-sized bungalow with a cellar below (and a tower above). Dennis Gill lived part of his youth in the clock, on the side of Citadel Hill, between the historic fort and Brunswick Street.

Ye Olde Towne Clocke.

When I contacted Dennis, he was teaching sculpting at the Nova Scotia College of Art and Design. I invited him to meet me at his former hillside home. I had convinced a Citadel Hill official to come down the hill to unlock the clock. They were going to let Dennis and I explore a space he hadn't been in for more than thirty years. A nostalgic trip back in time.

We met at the door on the north side of the clock base. A lean man with short curly hair, Dennis struck me as thoughtful and mild-mannered. Sensing radio's need for detailed descriptions, Dennis took me on a verbal journey into his past.

"On the side entrance, there was a closed-in porch that held things like garbage cans and my mother's wringer washer," Dennis begins.

We unlock the white wooden winter door and it creaks open. We step into a large sunlit room on the hill side of the clock building. The ceiling tile is mostly missing. A load of old lumber lays against the orange wall. There is a sooty kitchen sink and counter in the corner. Cupboards without doors. "Dusty, empty and unused," sums up my first impression. A clock that time forgot? Well, Dennis didn't forget.

"Directly in front of us was where our oil stove sat."

We move through a doorway to the front room. A curtainless window overlooks the traffic on Brunswick Street.

"Looking through this window, I'm reminded of one occasion when I was about six years old, walking home with some new chums. They were talking about where they lived and I said, 'Well I live in the clock.' And they said, 'Nobody lives in a clock. You can't live in the clock.' I said, 'Oh yes I do. I really do live in the clock.' When I got to the steps, I started walking up and they realized I was telling the truth and a couple of the older guys decided to beat me up." Dennis laughs. I suppose he got his clock cleaned. We move into a small room at the front of the building, behind the locked main entrance.

"My dad referred to this room as the 'reception room.' It's the area that the general public came to if they wanted a tour of the clock tower. One of the things that my father was responsible for was providing tours of the clock because it was an historic site. When tourists came to the door he'd have to get up and take them through the clock." A tourist's trip through time. Upon request! Dennis' father worked in a clock but he didn't keep regular hours. We shuffle through the small reception room into a larger room, well lit by the window facing the harbour.

"We're at the far end of the clock now. With a working fireplace. When we first moved here, the clock was heated with coal—and apparently had a very unreliable furnace. On many occasions my dad would get up in the night and have to shut everything down because the whole clock would be filled with coal smoke." Dennis is remembering through the smoky haze of time. He's enjoying this tour. Listen! Up above, the clock chimes. The sound filters down through the wooden floorboards of three storeys. Its lovely. We pause to let the sound sink in. It feels odd, this walk through a clock. But it's pleasant.

Out a rear window we see the old fort on top of the hill where young people in period costume fire off Halifax's famous gun everyday at noon. The cannon blast is done with blanks, not balls. It's for the tourists. But it is loud. Very loud. The blast reverberates daily in the downtown streets. Every day at noon sharp, office workers blocks away spill their coffee when the gun sounds. So I ask Dennis about the hazards of living under the gun, so to speak.

"Depending on the wind direction, quite often the repercussions from the noon-day gun would break a window pane. I have these memories of—certainly on a bi-weekly basis at times—workmen coming down from the Citadel to replace a pane of glass." Shoot the breeze, kill some time. I'd never thought those expressions could literally fit together. Dennis leads the way up inside the clock tower itself.

"We are climbing up a ladder at a 47-degree angle; somewhat reminiscent of steps that you find on a boat," says Dennis. "It certainly felt that steep when I was a child." Dennis and I reach the first level, a bright, many-sided chamber, mostly of windows. Outside it's surrounded by white pillars supporting the next level. We are facing what looks like a set of glass doors on a very tall grandfather clock.

"This door is probably fourteen feet tall," says Dennis. The glass door is wide open. Looking down inside the deep darkness of this pendulum closet makes me dizzy. It's a bottomless drop from the floor's edge. "Not a safe place for kids to play," I'm thinking.

"I was probably six years old the last time I opened this door," says Dennis, reading my mind.

"I had snuck out of the kitchen and made my way through the reception room and upstairs. When we open the door you'll notice that now there's two sticks across to prevent exactly what my mother was probably concerned about. It's a long drop down. Directly in front of me is the main pendulum and the clock counterweights."

We stop talking and listen. The beautiful, slow, heavy rhythm of the pendulum swing has a deep tock, tock sound. A feeling of comfort. The sound of security. It makes you sleepy. *Tock. Tock… Tock. Tock… Tock. Tock…*

"Yeah, pretty nice really. Imagine being in the city and having that kind of sound… it's like people who put clocks under pillows for young animals so that they can go to sleep." A "sound" sleep in more ways than one.

"I had a wonderful feeling of security when I lived here. I was a kid in a very historic structure without realizing how that structure appeared to other people." People in glass houses shouldn't throw stones. Apparently people who live in clock houses don't throw anything.

We're making the last climb up into the clock tower housing itself. Dennis describes the scene. "There's a wooden box with two glass doors. Front and back. It looks like a cross between a sarcophagus and a jewelry cabinet. Maybe that's appropriate. We see this wonderful cast-iron and bronze wind-up clock through the glass. The only time I could come up here was when my father had to change the hands of the clock for daylight savings time. Sometimes the whole family would come up and watch my father and a man from the Citadel work together—one of them would have to go outside on a catwalk and physically turn the hands of the clock. It was a family affair, setting the clock."

How many people can make a statement like that? Most families would get ticked off. We climb up to one last level. This stairway is steeper. The chambers are getting smaller. At the top I hear the noise of traffic. We are outside now, in the open belfry of the old town clock. The domed roof with the ball on top is overhead. But this space is open to the air.

Dennis the tour guide takes over. "Okay Bruce, here we are on the roof of the clock tower. We're in the belfry and we're looking out directly down George Street and over the rooftops and out toward McNab's Island to the south. Three wonderful bells of three different sizes, obviously producing different tones. This is the roof of my old home! To be back here now, to be walking through it brings to mind those very early experiences that could only, I realize now, be triggered by having climbed the tower. It's an emotional experience for me."

What a fun place to be as a kid, living in a clock. It's Disneyesque. Much more fun than living in a shoe. Or in a pumpkin. Dennis' family lived under the bells, and there they kept him very well. Atop of the historic town clock, I look at my watch. It's almost two. We hurry down the steep stairs before the bells go off. One level down, we wait in silence for the minutes to tick by. It's quiet. Suddenly, a creak of old wood and the sound of a big, soft gong fills the shaft of the tower.

Bing, Bong, Bing. Bong! Bong!

The bell sound is full and spongy in the tower's wooden chamber. A subtle echo remains in our ears for a few seconds. It's beautiful. We want to keep it in our hearts. For a long minute Dennis Gill reflects on his trip back in time.

"This has been wonderful. Of course the longer I stay here, the more memories come to mind. Things I haven't thought of in twenty- or thirty-some years. The clock for me represents a kind of talisman, or keepsake that brings back a flood of memories. I was thinking how that sounded thirty-five years ago. It sounds every bit as exciting as I remember it. Time is a physical thing for me. Yeah, time is a physical thing."

Halifax's Bad Luck Birth

How the French induced the British to prematurely deliver our provincial capital.

Interesting history can result when bad things happen to good places. Consider our capital city, Nova Scotia's thriving gateway since 1749. Halifax was founded by bad luck. The city is a fair phoenix that rose from the flames of chaos, confusion, and death.

Three years prior to the celebrated landing of our capital city's British founder, Edward Cornwallis, another sort of expedition set forth for our shores. It was huge. But it was from France. Now wait, don't tune out. Yes we're dipping into those interminable seesawing, French-English power struggles that baffled us in high school history. But this is a plot. It was actually the French who founded our British garrison town—sort of. The French were on a mission in 1746. The British had just taken Louisbourg away from them the previous year. In the established New World tradition of seesaw warfare, France wanted revenge. Tit for tat. Leading this most massive of all New World French naval expeditions was a guy with a massive name: Jean-Baptiste Louis Frédéric de La Rochefoucauld de Roye.

You might know him by his simple title, the Duc d'Anville. There's a school by that name in Halifax. I learned about the Duc d'Anville's tragically unlucky adventures from a visiting historian. Professor James Pritchard wrote the book, *Anatomy of a Naval Disaster: The 1746 French Expedition to North America.* The author and I sat on a wooden bench on Citadel Hill, overlooking the harbour where d'Anville's ships arrived, over 250 years ago. The professor told me the French king instructed the Duc d'Anville to seek revenge at any cost.

"Louis XV told him that if he couldn't take Louisbourg, he'd better take an equivalent. And the equivalent was either Nova Scotia or Placentia, Newfoundland. Or if he could swing it, burning Boston wouldn't be too bad either!"

Pritchard laughed. "So his orders were broadly given."

If his orders were vague, the Duc's naval skills were fuzzier. He was, "utterly inexperienced and loathed by the French naval officer core," said Pritchard. "He was a Courtier Admiral. He came from the aristocracy and had never been in a sailing warship in his life." Oops. Foremen should never try to be managers. It gets worse. This incompetent commander was put in charge of a floating city of sailors and soldiers. The Duc d'Anville's fleet was focussed around ten naval warships with about sixty guns each. The numbers involved were amazing.

"It was accompanied by about fourteen troop ships carrying about thirty-five hundred officers and men, including four battalions of regular French line-infantry. A special naval battalion also accompanied the warships. There were thirteen or fourteen provision ships, and I haven't even mentioned the frigates, corvettes, and smaller warships that came along. In total, more than eleven thousand men left France in about sixty-four ships." Like I said, a floating city. Actually it was like three amalgamated cities under one leader. A concept clearly too awkward to work! Bad luck set in. A French farce followed.

King Louis' armada was formed to counter a British expedition that was cancelled at the last minute. British prerogative. Word came too late for the French—they were already under sail. Next, off Sable Island, a hurricane hit. One vessel was grounded leaving its crew stranded on Sable for a year. Disease struck the crews of the other ships. Burials at sea became routine. French fighting strength was cut by forty per cent. Only forty-two of the original sixty-four ships limped into our harbour. Four thousand men had died. The fleet moored at the harbour mouth, off McNab's Island. Then things got worse.

The Duc d'Anville, who should have had his head examined, developed a brain tumour. He died on the job. Some say he died of his doctor's ministrations. The naval surgeon gave the patient an enema, two blood-lettings and induced vomiting. D'Anville was buried on George's Island, in the very harbour he came to claim. His second-in-command took charge. But stress does funny things to sailors and he threw himself on his own sword. Next up for the position was Monsieur De La Jonquierre. Third time lucky, the expedition finally had a reliable leader, a capable sea captain.

Captain De La Jonquierre took the ships into Bedford Basin, a great "stopping place," according to its highway sign. But the fleet's bad luck didn't change there. A typhoid and typhus epidemic claimed more men. From our Citadel perch Professor Pritchard looked over the basin and continued his tale of pathos.

"Twelve hundred sailors had died by the time the French finally left. Their corpses lined the shore of Birch Cove in Bedford Basin. They didn't even try to make an encampment." The terrible disease also decimated the local Mi'kmaq population.

La Jonquierre ordered the fleet to sail around to Annapolis Royal. Perhaps they could seize control of the Port. Nope. They met another hurricane off Nova Scotia's tip. And disease struck again. More death! Finally, their ships turned towards home, dogged by attacking British ships along the way. Several thousand more died on the return trip. Of the original eleven thousand who left France, only two thousand returned. Not a good return on investment. If the French effort had succeeded, today Halifax might be known for its escargot instead of its donairs.

"It was because of the d'Anville expedition that Halifax was established three years later," said Professor Pritchard. "Halifax is the only city in North America ever founded by the British government. Every other English city on this continent was founded by British merchants, settlers or religious refugees, but never by the British government."

Now *that* I didn't know. The French gave the Brits a wake-up call. Or you might say that French midwives induced the British into labour, and delivered a healthy new colonial town a little earlier than expected.

The historic Citadel overlooks the harbour island where Duc d'Anville met his tragic end.

"Suddenly," said the professor, "the British Navy's pleas to establish a settlement resounded with a great crash. Yes, they better do something, and Cornwallis was sent to Halifax shortly thereafter."

Hence, Halifax—born of bad luck.

The Great Explosion Question

A unique perspective on what happened minutes before Nova Scotia's worst disaster.

Eighty-some years afterwards, we all know the "what," "where," and "when" of the Halifax Explosion. But, why? Why did two ships, moving slowly, on a bright, sunny morning, with plenty of room to pass each other, collide?

Captain Bob Power has a theory about the "why" of the collision, based on his twenty-four years of piloting those harbour narrows. He has also read the transcripts of the formal inquiry that investigated the big blast. His theory hangs on three hooks: the harbour's shape, the vessel *Imo*'s mechanics, and the sun's location. Here's my summary of Captain Power's informed speculation:

First, Halifax Harbour is not straight. As the narrow harbour channel empties into the round Bedford Basin, there's about a thirty-degree bend to the left. That's why the *Imo*, a 440-foot-long vessel coming *out* of the basin into the harbour Narrows, had to first point her bow towards Dartmouth, then swing it the opposite way toward Halifax. Literally she went "round the bend."

It was a tight turn for a cumbersome ship. Then, as she awkwardly pivoted, a tug passed illegally on her starboard side. (That's the right side although the tug was on the wrong side.) That may have caused *Imo* to delay her turn. Captain Power told me *Imo* then came astern, that is, threw her engine into reverse to slow *and* turn her simultaneously—a perfectly reasonable manoeuvre.

Inquiry testimony suggests the *Imo* then killed her engine at the entrance to the narrows as though to avoid something ahead, but still drifted forward.

Pretend it is the morning of December 6, 1917. You're the captain on board the munitions ship, *Mont Blanc*. You are sailing up an unfamiliar harbour, close to the Dartmouth shore. You see a long ship in your path. She's in mid-pivot. Her engines are stopped but she is drifting forward towards you.

Switch. You are at the helm on board the pivoting *Imo*. The sun is eighteen degrees above the horizon and shooting into your eyes through a haze of coal smoke. Where is the ship you were warned was approaching? Suddenly, the *Mont Blanc* appears! The oncoming ship—loaded with explosives—is now turning hard toward Halifax, breaking the nautical convention of keeping to the right when a collision is imminent. (Her captain said later he thought the starboard waters too shallow to go hard-right.) *Imo* rips into Mont Blanc's starboard side. Fire erupts aboard the *Mont Blanc*. Her captain and crew, aware of her dangerous cargo, jump ship. Like a giant floating stick of dynamite, the abandoned *Mont Blanc* drifts toward the Halifax docks and grinds ashore. The flames leap higher. As the *Mont Blanc* incinerates, Halifax residents watch the fire from their windows, fascinated by the flames.

Minutes later, the exploding ship flattens most of the city's North End. And all because the captain of the *Imo* had the sun in his eyes and the captain of the *Mont Blanc* was making an illegal left turn. One ship's captain was affected by the brightness—the other captain made a move that wasn't very bright at all.

Halifax Harbour today.

A Lighthouse in a Bowl

*The psychic saviour of Seal Island
starts our first life-saving station.*

This is a true-life adventure of a remarkable Nova Scotian woman. It's a story of vision, courage, determination, dedication and fearless opposition to nature's wrath—all in the name of compassion for shipwrecked sailors. The account of this great adventure opens with my tiny misadventure. Note the contrast.

I was on the road. It felt good to get out of the city, away from the stale air of the CBC Radio building. I was headed to a place with a dramatic history, where long ago brave people did amazing things. That's not to say that dramatic things don't happen in the CBC Radio building. They do. Live radio can be fraught with crisis. And the brave people there cope well. But those are the troubles of the airwaves. This is a tale of trouble on the ocean waves.

I was invited by members of the Lighthouse Preservation Society of Nova Scotia to join a group of eighteen on an eighteen-mile voyage to lonely Seal Island, off the province's southern tip. It's a place ripe with rip tides and human adventure stretching back centuries. We were to sail out, bunk overnight in one of the fishermen's buildings, tour the old lighthouse and walk the shores. Spending the weekend on an isolated island, rich in Atlantic beauty and dramatic history would be thrilling. I leaped at the chance. I drove my car for three hours to Shelburne County, through Barrington, and over the short causeway to Cape Sable Island. From this island, the group of lighthouse lovers was to depart the next morning in one of the famous Cape Island fishing boats. We planned to sail to the historic Atlantic burial ground, Seal Island, at nine AM. The bed and breakfast was charming. The owners were the Atkinsons, relatives of the family that built the first Cape Islander.

Early next morning, I gulped seasickness pills with my coffee. By nine sharp I was at the end of the wharf, in the whipping wind, waiting to meet my hosts. It was a foggy, cold and blustery September morning. Being a realist, I was fully prepared to endure the two-hour boat trip hanging over the side. I knew what I was in for. I had been warned. Even experienced fishermen lose their lunch. Or, in this case, their breakfast. It's a middle ear thing. The last time I had been out in rough seas, miles from the coast, in a small bobbing boat was… never. But I figured a bit of seasickness was the cost of doing business. As a matter of fact, my stomach was already rolling from looking at the bobbing boats. A little anticipatory nausea. Still, I was willing. However, I was alone. I looked at my watch. Ten past nine. Where was everybody? A young fisherman in a ball cap pulled up in his pickup. He was the captain of our groups' transport vessel. But he looked more like a messenger. The trip was cancelled. The lighthouse lovers didn't like the look of the weather. I was the only one there. A broken-hearted man at the end of a pier. How I wished I were on Seal Isle now. The captain was game. He looked at the choppy waters and rubbed his chin. "Looks calm to me. I woulda gone." "Me too," I said, ignoring the protests of my head and stomach and the side effects of Gravol. "Yeah, I'd do it," I confirmed, in too loud a voice. (Methinks the laddie pretends too much.) I thanked the boat owner and staggered to my car, bracing against the driving wind and salt spray. Hmm. Was that relief I was feeling? No, it must be the drug.

What now? The rental car, the B & B and a gross of Gravol cost a pretty penny. I needed to bring back *something* to placate my producer. I needed an instant inspiration. The rental car had to be back before dark. I flipped through my copy of *Light in the Darkness*. I had picked up this Seal Island history the day before, at the Barrington Woollen Mill Museum. I'd stopped there out of curiosity, to take a peek at the huge fabric mural hanging in the large loft. It featured the first woven sample of blue Nova Scotia tartan, sewn into the kilt of a tiny Highland shepherd. An historic scrap of cloth, whose story appears elsewhere in this book. So, I thought I'd finally find out what I was talking about. (You know what I mean.)

The book was written by Walter Hichens, the great-great-grandson of Seal Island's original settlers. He was already a senior when he wrote the book years earlier. Hichens' bio on the back claimed he was a retired state senator who lived in Maine. "What are my chances of getting in touch with him?" I asked myself. I had asked my contact at the museum the same question. It was a lucky question. I could feel it. As it happened, Senator Hichens was not only still living, he was living just down the road, at his summer house. He was eighty-four years old and leaving for Maine in two days.

Walter Hichens' voice was gravelly but not gruff on the pay phone. He invited me to the breakfast he was cooking for his wife. I drove down the road and pulled in behind the car with the Maine licence plates. The stone foundation on the 150-year-old house was crumbling at the corners. The white paint was cracked and blistered. The grass needed mowing. I lifted the latch and was welcomed into the old house which smelled of must, dust, and worn wooden floors. An old-fashioned stove warmed the large kitchen. Mr. Hichens looked like your average American state senator—a shock of grey hair, thick black-framed glasses, wearing a white shirt, open at the collar, with sleeves rolled. At eighty-four, he moved slowly but confidently. This great former states-man and author was preparing scrambled eggs for his wife, a victim of Alzheimer's disease. He put her plate in front of her and placed a fork in her hand. A moment of true poignancy. Only an hour before, I was anticipating an exhilarating ocean voyage. Now I was sitting in a comfortable kitchen watching one of life's truly dramatic moments.

The setting was appropriate. Walter Hichens' story of Seal Island is ancient, like the house itself. It's about a strong, selfless person. It's about the saviour of Seal Island, Walter Hichens' great-great-grand-mother, Mary Hichens.

Mary's passion to help the hopeless came to her in a dream. A nightmare really. In 1820, while Mary was living on the mainland, she began having terrifying visions, fuelled, most likely, by local fishermen's stories of marine disasters at Seal Island. Mary would often awaken thinking she had heard the screams of drowning people.

"One year, one of the fishermen came back," the senator began, "and told how they found a body beside a stove he had tried to build. He died there, froze to death and she got so worked up about it that she started having dreams about all these wrecks. She was sort of clairvoyant I guess, because she would wake up in the night and say, 'There's someone dying out there in the ocean.' When she got married, her husband got so disturbed about it he didn't know what to do."

Walter watched his wife atten-
tively as he spoke. Their relationship seemed strong but strained by
the infirmities of old age.

Wreck of *Columbia Steamship*.

In the early 1820s, Mary Hichens' relationship with her new spouse was also difficult, but for different reasons. Her husband was confused by her wild dreams and her sudden decision to move out to Seal Island to save shipwreck victims. They had married in February 1820. Mary Hichens had been Mary Crowell, a minister's daughter. One night she had a vision of the vessel *Friendship* sinking off Seal Island. Mary insisted that men go out to the island to save the sailors of *Friendship*. She must have been a very persuasive woman to get fishermen out of their beds in the middle of the night for a bad dream. But her nightmarish vision was all too real. The vessel was going down. Sailors scrambled for their lives. The fishermen Mary sent out must have been astonished to see a bad dream come true. One of the sailors rescued off

Seal Island was the captain Richard Hichens. He recuperated at Mary's house. They fell in love and were married—the sailor and his saviour.

So it probably didn't take Mary long to persuade her new husband to move out to the island. "She says, 'Well, you wouldn't be here if somebody hadn't rescued you,'" said Walter. By that time, they had two little boys. Nevertheless, Richard and Mary Hichens made the move. They went to live on Seal Island where so many had died tragically in years gone by.

Thomas H. Raddall describes Seal Island in a November 1948 article written for the *Saturday Evening Post*. The celebrated Nova Scotian writer accomplished what I didn't; he sailed to Seal Island and explored its history firsthand. Raddall writes:

"For three centuries Seal Island was a fatal trap for ships caught in the fog or storm or the powerful Fundy tidal rip on the passage around Cape Sable. The graves of drowned sailors are everywhere on the island which is less than three miles long and roughly half a mile wide. No land is more than forty feet above sea level and a dense tangle of scrub spruce covers all of the island except the low dunes and a few acres of salt marsh. Along the west side, where the winter wind cuts like a sword across the mouth of the Fundy, the trees are gnarled and twisted."

The Hichens went to live on that rugged little island to offer food, shelter, and assistance to shipwrecked survivors. Our modern-day coast guard claims that during the first thirteen years that the Hichens lived on Seal Isle, there were ninety-five ships wrecked on its shoals and sand bars. The Hichens did what they could to limit the number of deaths. They developed a precursor to the lighthouse now on the island. They knew that seal oil would fuel a lighted wick, so they put it to clever use.

"They would take the oil and put it in little bowls," said Walter, "and put the lighted bowls on the rocks, all around, in case there was a shipwreck, so that any surviving sailors would know that there was some hope there, you know, that there was some help."

A lighthouse in a bowl. Very clever, Mary Hichens.

Mary had her life-saving work cut out for her. Walter nodded to a large framed chart on the wall that showed what his great-great grandmother was up against. The map of Seal Island shipwrecks showed a group of tiny islands of which Seal Isle is the largest. All around the oddly shaped islands are clusters of sinking-ship symbols: schooners and steamships and barques and barquentines and brigs and brigantines. The Hichens kept a record of the wrecks, but it too is lost. There is no formal count of lives saved or lives lost. Suffice to say that hundreds died. Yet hundreds were saved. Ships on the great sea route between Cape Cod and Europe foundered on Seal Island's outlying reefs—Blonde Rock, Loch Foyne Shoal, Scratch All, The Devil's Limb, Hospital Rip, South Bar, and Mother Owen's Rock. The first explorer to see and record Seal Island was the famous Samuel de Champlain. He sailed around the dangerous island with de Monts in 1604, four years before his trip up the St. Lawrence River when he founded Quebec. Champlain noted the abundance of seals and called it *Ile aux Loups Marins*. He also wrote of the vast array of bird life: cormorants, geese, ducks of three kinds, sea parrots, snipes, vultures, herons, sea larks, kites, crows, crane, and other sorts. Feathered friends in a desolate place. Later, a flock of sheep was brought to the island to provide meat to feed lucky survivors of wrecks who struggled ashore.

This was Mary and her husband's new home. They were not alone on the island. Edmund Crowell, Mary's brother, and his wife, Jerusha, settled there with them. The two families built houses on opposite shores of the island, close enough that the chimney smoke from one home was a visible comfort to the other. As he poured me more coffee, Walter told me of one of his visits to "his" island when he was researching his great-great-grandparents' life adventures. He recorded the oral history from another descendant of the pioneer Hichens and Crowells.

Winifred Hamilton, great-granddaughter of Edmund Crowell, eventually inherited the island. She lived her entire life on Seal Island, subsisting on a meagre income garnered from local fishermen who were willing to pay a small annual fee to dock and bunk on the island during fishing seasons. This daughter and widow of lightkeepers was born about 1890. Walter had walked the island shores with Winifred Hamilton. He carefully documented her memories of the island families and their stories. Recording those memories was a labour of love for Walter. He wrote and published what he was told, so that love's labour was not lost. I felt as though he were handing me his child when he gave me his family history to retell on radio. It was his gift to Nova Scotia. Walter reached across the table for my copy of his book. He wanted to sign it. To leave his mark.

Seal Island's light was a triumph that came from a determined lobby. Mary Hichens was the driving force. As women had no political rights at the time, Mary first lobbied her husband who, in turn, wrote to the Governor-General, Sir James Kempt. The following summer, the old

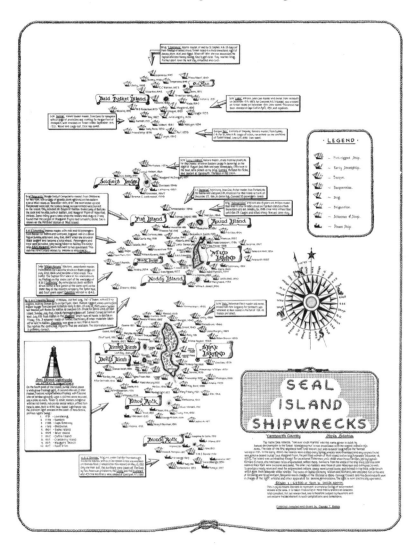

veteran of Waterloo came in a naval brig to see the place for himself. The wreckage and graves that littered the shore line told their own tale. In the summer of 1831, Mary and Richard Hichens got their lighthouse. The colonial government of Nova Scotia erected the light on a knoll at the southern tip of the island. It was massive and sturdy, built of rough timbers. A modern lamp with revolving lenses was fitted on top. Like Mary Hichens' signal bowls, the new lighthouse would burn seal oil.

Mary Hichens' connection to that symbolic light was personal and emotional. It was the goal she had worked towards during all of those years of witnessing so much tragedy on the island—tragedy she foresaw in her nightmares before even setting foot on the island. So it was prophetic that Mary gave birth on the day the light was to be lit. Mary insisted on attending the lighting, despite her condition. Walter retold the 166-year-old family story:

"She wanted to go into the lighthouse but they knew that she wouldn't be able to climb the stairs. But when Richard saw them coming up the lane he ran down to tell them that the doctor said it was all right. So they took her to the lighthouse builder's room where she would have a view of the light. It was just as the baby was being born that Mary saw the light go out across the ocean. That was the first baby born on Seal Island."

The baby saw the first light of day as sailors skirting the shore saw the first light at night. Mary's spirit must have soared that day. She gave new life to her baby and to countless seafarers who would be guided safely by the light. Symbolism knows no bounds.

Mary's baby was the first born on the island, but she and the Crowells had already had children when they moved there. The older Crowell children had perhaps the most gripping experience of the family. One November day the Hichens and Crowells left the island to make a quick trip to the mainland for supplies before the winter gales hit. The Crowells' three children, all under twelve, didn't care to sail the tossing waves and were permitted to stay behind on the island. The parents would, after all, return soon. Unexpectedly, a fierce Nova Scotia storm blew up and, according to oral history, it heralded an entire winter of bitter, blustery, unsailable weather. The three Crowell children, one twelve, one nine, one seven, were marooned. Alone.

"The three youngsters survived the whole winter by themselves on the island," said Walter. "They killed ducks for meat and they'd walk down every couple of days to the Hichens' place on the other coast to milk the cow and gather eggs from the hens. Unfortunately, the youngest boy got quite sick with a cold; aside from that they survived the winter quite well. In the spring of 1825 they saw their father coming back to get them." Parents reading this may now exhale. Imagine being ashore for weeks and months while your kids are stranded in wild isolation. Fear and worry would be constant. And yet a comforting voice sustained the Crowells waiting out the winter on the mainland. Mary Hichens reassured her friends that their children were fine. She could see them with her visionary eye. Again, Mary reached out and offered hope during hopeless times.

So, the Hichens and the Crowells became synonymous with the rich history of Seal Island. The fabric of their families is woven into the rugged tapestry of that wonderful, dangerous place. And it became part of them. Mary Hichens set up the first private life-saving station in North America; her sons grew up and stayed for a time on the island. They built lifeboats of their own design. The Royal Humane Society in far-away England sent a set of life preservers. After her husband died, Mary left the island to her children and moved to Cape Cod, Massachusetts where she lived out her final days. Mary's children eventually moved to the mainland. Descendants of the Crowells lived and worked on Seal Island throughout the 1800s and through much of this century.

Local fishermen still use the island as a stopover, guided by the lighthouse beacon that is still in operation. Mary Hichens' name lives on, immortalized on a Canadian Coast Guard search-and-rescue vessel named for her. Her name is etched proudly on the prow, just as it is forever etched in the thoughts of her great, great grandson who proudly attended the christening of CCGS *Mary Hichens*.

Walter cleared away the breakfast plates from the table. I handed him my coffee cup and thanked him for telling me Mary Hichens' story, and for the experience of hearing it in that wonderful old house. It was special. It brought life to the story that a trip to the island wouldn't have. I said goodbye to Walter and his wife and walked out the front door, back into present time.

CCGS *Mary Hichens* continues her namesake's tradition of saving sailors in trouble at sea.

Selecteð Bibliography

Avery, Oswald T., Colin M. McLeod, and MacLyn McCarty. "Studies on the Chemical Nature of Substance Inducing Transformation of Pneumococcal Types: Induction of Transformation by a Deoxyribonucleic Acid Fraction Isolated from Pneumococcus Type 3." *Journal of Experimental Medicine.* Nov. (1943).

Borrett, William C. *Historic Halifax in Tales Told Under the Old Town Clock.* Toronto: Ryerson Press, 1948.

Brown, R. J. "Alexander Graham Bell and the Garfield Assassination." *Newspapers Collectors Society of America* (Newsletter) Aug. (1997).

Burton, Pierre. *Klondike: The Last Great Gold Rush 1896-1899.* Toronto: McClelland & Stewart, 1972.

Day, Phillip. "Stone of Scone Returns Home, Fishermen Used as Spies." *Halifax Chronicle-Herald* Nov. 1996, n. d., n. pag.

Dubos, René. *The Professor, the Institute and DNA: Oswald T. Avery, His Life and Scientific Achievements.* New York: Rockefeller University Press, 1961.

Gillen, Mollie. *The Prince and His Lady: The Love Story of the Duke of Kent and Madame de St. Laurent.* London: Sidgwick and Jackson, 1970.

Gray, Michael. "DNA and Heredity: 1944 Paper Caused Little Hype." *Dalhousie News* 16 Feb. 1994.

Grant, Francis. "When the Wind Shifted Suddenly, the Squall and Disaster Occurred." *The Strait News.* 3 June 1976.

Hichens, Walter W. *Light in the Darkness: Highlights from the Life of Mary Hichens, Heroine of Seal Island.* Hantsport, NS: Lancelot Press, 1993.

Ingalls, Sharon. "The Duke's Romantic Retreat." *The Beaver.* June-July (1996): 29-36.

MacDonald, David. "Nova Scotia's Wacky Nicknames." *Reader's Digest.* Oct. 1980. 13.

Major, Marjorie. *How Nova Scotia Got Its Tartan.* Reprinted from *The Nova Scotia Historical Quarterly* 2.2. Halifax: McCurdy Printing, 1972.

Matheson, Trueman. *A History of Londonderry Nova Scotia.* Truro, NS: Phoenix Press Ltd., 1983.

McDade, Garnet. *The McDade Family: Three Generations.* Kentville, NS: McDade private papers, Kentville, 1983.

MacKenzie, A. A. "Do You Know Sandy Red Rory Big Rory The Flea?" *The Clansman Magazine,* June–July 1992.

Newcomb, Simon. *The Reminiscences of an Astronomer.* London: 1903.

Nova Scotia. *An Act Respecting the Nova Scotia Tartan,* Chapt. 318 of RSNS, 1989. Amended O.I.C. 90-987.

Parker, John P. *Sails of the Maritimes: The Story of the Three- and Four-Masted Cargo Schooners of Atlantic Canada 1859–1929.* Toronto: McGraw Hill Ryerson, 1960.

Payzant, Joan and Aaron Solomon. "Radio Pioneer Joe Fassett Still Fondly Remembered; Part Two, Radio Pioneers of Dartmouth." *Dartmouth Free Press*, 7 Nov. 1979.

Poitras, Jacques. "Nova Scotia Town Finds Spot in Soviet History." *Moncton Times-Transcript* 6 Aug. 1988: 10.

Poundstone, William. "Newcomb's Paradox." In *Labyrinths of Reason*. n. d. pub. unknown.

Preston, Diana. *The Road to Culloden Moor: Bonnie Prince Charlie and the '45 Rebellion.* London: Constable Ltd., 1995.

Pritchard, James. *Anatomy of a Naval Disaster.* Montreal and Kingston: McGill-Queen's University Press, 1995.

Pringle, David. *Imaginary People: Who's Who of Fictional Characters from the 18th Century to the Present Day.* 2nd ed. London: Ashgate Publishing, 1996.

Raddall, Thomas. "Island for Sale." *The Saturday Evening Post* 16 Nov. 1948.

Raddall, Thomas. "Nova Scotia's First Telegraph System." *Dalhousie Review* (1947) 131-142.

Russell, W. Clark. *A Voyage at Anchor.* New York: D. Appleton and Co., 1899.

Wallace, Frederick William. *Record of Canadian Shipping: A List of Square Rigged Vessels, Mainly 50 Tons and Over, Built in the Eastern Provinces of British North America from the Year 1786 to 1920.* Toronto: The Musson Book Company Ltd.

Werner, Hans. "And What, Exactly, was Leon Trotsky Doing in Nova Scotia in 1917?" *Saturday Night*, Aug. 1974.

West, Bruce. "Meeting Great Minds at Canada's Place in the Sun." *Globe and Mail* 13 June 1972.

Wright, Allen. *Prelude to Bonanza: The Discovery and Exploration of the Yukon.* Sydney, BC: Gray's Publishing Ltd., 1976.

Zeller, Suzanne and Gale Avrith-Wakeam. "Dawson, George." *Dictionary of Canadian Biography.* Vol. 12, 1990.

"After 700 Year Wait, Scots Welcome Stone of Scone Home." *Globe and Mail*, Nov. 1996.

"A Hero of the Seas." *The Life Boat: The Journal of the Royal National Life-Boat Institution* 23. No. 257 (1915).

"Annual Culloden Memorial Service Held." *The Casket* Antigonish, 13 May 1995.

"Capt. McDade Passes Away at New York." *The Halifax Herald*, 23 May 1933: 3.

"John Fassett, 72, Dies." *The New York Times*, 10 March 1996.

"Macdonald, Flora." *Dictionary of National Biography* Vol. 12 (1922).

"The Man Behind Moriarty." *Sky and Telescope*, June, 1993: 11-12.

Bibliographical Note

The selected bibliography above does not include references to personal interviews which are referred to in the body of this book. Also, because these stories were originally researched for radio, not all bibliographical information was recorded—particularly where material was mailed, faxed or photocopied by librarians or experts in particular fields who vouched for the value and accuracy of the written material. Therefore, authors' names, publishers, or dates of publication are not listed in some cases. Other reference material is omitted entirely from this list because bibliographical information was not recorded.

Author's Footnote to Bibliographical Note

It's not that I'm lazy. I didn't record bibliographical information in every case because I was telling stories on radio. I never planned to write a book...but I'm glad I did.